PRAISE FOR *STRIVE TOGETHER*

[Strive Together is] a must-read for business leaders, educators, coaches, and anyone pursuing excellence in their lives. Jeff Moore is a true original, a contrarian visionary who has developed a revolutionary approach to helping leaders tackle the complex problems they face in rapidly changing environments. Jeff's concept of "Strivership" has helped my athletes understand the true meaning of competition, teaching them how to confront themselves, their teammates, and yes, even their coaches, all in an effort to become a championship team.

—Geoff McDonald

Head coach, Vanderbilt Women's Tennis (2015 NCAA Champions)

I have never heard anyone articulate the principles I believe in the way Jeff did when I heard his presentation and Q&A at our UNC Leadership Academy. Jeff understands that "competing" is based on the Latin origin "to strive together." [Competition] can be a critical platform for development, especially when people are driven by a purpose that transcends winning. Listening to him was an education, confirming what I have always dedicated my life to and introducing me to excellent ideas for improving the way I do things now.

—Anson Dorrance

World Champion Coach, USA
Twenty-two-time national champion coach, University of North Carolina

I highly recommend this book to any leader who wants to build a championship team. Jeff's work can be a game changer for organizations seeking to thrive in a rapid-change environment, and his approach resonates with every generation!

—Jimmy Treybig

Founder and CEO, Tandem Computers

There are many books written on leadership, but few that are as thought-provoking as this work. In Strive Together, *Jeff addresses the importance of understanding excellence in leadership, but also, and perhaps more importantly, discusses ways to cultivate excellence.* Strive Together *provides educators with an approach to engaging young people [in a way] that prepares them to thrive when confronted with the ever-mounting challenges of a disruptive real world.*

—Kevin Moore

Cofounder, Long-View School

Jeff Moore recovers the true meaning of competition—to strive together—in this winsome and practical guide to building successful teams. Based on his experience coaching athletes to peak performance, Moore's approach to inspiring players, instilling accountability, and celebrating accomplishment applies immediately to any situation where we need to bring out the best in each other. Moore's take on leadership is fresh and challenging. It's as if he sees business as a game where the real payoff is wholehearted community.

—Steven Tomlinson

Master teacher, Acton School of Business

STRIVE
TOGETHER

JEFF MOORE

STRIVE TOGETHER

ACHIEVE BEYOND EXPECTATIONS IN A RESULTS-OBSESSED WORLD

Published by Advantage, Charleston, South Carolina.
Member of Advantage Media Group.

ADVANTAGE is a registered trademark, and the Advantage colophon is a trademark of Advantage Media Group, Inc.

Printed in the United States of America.

10 9 8 7 6 5 4 3 2 1

ISBN: 978-1-64225-029-9
LCCN: 2019911368

Book design by Megan Elger.

This publication is designed to provide accurate and authoritative information in regard to the subject matter covered. It is sold with the understanding that the publisher is not engaged in rendering legal, accounting, or other professional services. If legal advice or other expert assistance is required, the services of a competent professional person should be sought.

 Advantage Media Group is proud to be a part of the Tree Neutral® program. Tree Neutral offsets the number of trees consumed in the production and printing of this book by taking proactive steps such as planting trees in direct proportion to the number of trees used to print books. To learn more about Tree Neutral, please visit **www.treeneutral.com**.

Advantage Media Group is a publisher of business, self-improvement, and professional development books and online learning. We help entrepreneurs, business leaders, and professionals share their Stories, Passion, and Knowledge to help others Learn & Grow. Do you have a manuscript or book idea that you would like us to consider for publishing? Please visit **advantagefamily.com** or call **1.866.775.1696**.

To my father, who modeled what it means to lead by being led, and to my mother, who inspired me with her relentlessly optimistic view of life.

TABLE OF CONTENTS

ACKNOWLEDGMENTS XI

ABOUT THE AUTHOR XIII

PART ONE
Striving Together

INTRODUCTION 3

CHAPTER ONE. 5
Big Shoes to Fill

CHAPTER TWO 25
The True Meaning of Competition

CHAPTER THREE 43
The Power of Strivership

CHAPTER FOUR 69
Why Strivership Matters

CHAPTER FIVE 81
The Striver Quotient® Assessment

PART TWO
Building Championship Teams

CHAPTER SIX **99**
Lead by Being Led

CHAPTER SEVEN **115**
Building Championship Companies

CHAPTER EIGHT **135**
Building Championship Teams in Sports

CHAPTER NINE **167**
Imbuing a Spirit of Strivership in Schools

CALL TO ACTION **181**

ACKNOWLEDGMENTS

Writing this book has been a humbling experience. I am grateful to so many people for their contributions and support. This project has been a team effort.

The people at Advantage Media Group|ForbesBooks provided invaluable expertise, guidance, and support throughout the process. Bea Wray showed confidence in my ideas by reaching out to me two years ago about taking on this project. Keith Farrell was with me every step of the way and his writing expertise was invaluable. He helped me breathe life into these pages. Eland Mann provided keen insights as my editor. He made several important recommendations, especially with respect to the structure and flow of the book. Megan Elger has unleashed her creative abilities on the design process and Adam Vlach managed all of the details required to get me over the finish line.

I have learned that knowing what you don't know is what fuels personal growth and development. For this reason, I have always tried to surround myself with peers who challenge my thinking. I thrive when I am engaging with people who are true disruptors in their industries.

Geoff McDonald and Paul Wardlaw, both former colleagues and good friends (and national championship coaches!) have challenged me throughout my career with their thought-provoking perspectives on coaching—which often seem to be coming out of left field until you reflect on them.

Kevin Moore is a visionary educator who has challenged me to reimagine education by thinking of teachers as cultivators of learning, not instructors. Kevin is a desperately needed disruptive force in an industry dominated by people who love to put outside-the-box thinking in a box.

Tony Capasso, Jimmy Treybig, and Jim Albrecht have challenged me by providing invaluable expertise and feedback as I have embarked on my new adventure into the business world. Their straightforward, unvarnished insights have been crucial to navigating what, for me, have been uncharted waters.

This project has been time consuming and self-absorbing. I am grateful for my wife, Lucy's, patience and support throughout the process. It is difficult enough to be married to a coach, much less a coach who dives into a book project!

My greatest debt is owed to my athletes at Redlands, Kent Denver, Colorado, Texas, and St. Stephens. Thank you for letting me play a small part in the many great stories that you have created. You taught me more than I ever could hope to teach you.

ABOUT THE AUTHOR

Jeff Moore is the CEO of Moore Leadership, LLC. He helps leaders in business and education build championship teams using the revolutionary Striver Quotient® Assessment Tool. During his career, his teams won two NCAA Championships, appeared in two NCAA finals, advanced to the NCAA Final Four three times, reached the NCAA Elite Eight three times, and won eighteen conference titles.

Jeff is a member of the Longhorn Hall of Honor and the College Tennis Hall of Fame. He has been named National Coach of the Year and was Conference Coach of the Year ten times. Before taking the reins at Texas, Jeff coached the men's and women's tennis teams at the University of Colorado. He began his career coaching women's basketball at the University of Redlands. Jeff served as chairperson of the NCAA Men's and Women's Tennis Committee and as a member of the Intercollegiate Tennis Association's board of directors. He also coached basketball at the Kent Denver School and St. Stephen's Episcopal School.

Jeff graduated from the University of Redlands and received his master's in education from the University of Texas. He and his wife, Lucy, reside in Austin, Texas. They have two boys living in Austin—

Tim, a dean at St. Andrews Episcopal School, and Andy, who works in product management for GoDaddy.

To learn more, visit http://www.mooreleadership.com/Home. aspx.

PART ONE

STRIVING TOGETHER

INTRODUCTION

We choose to go to the moon in this decade and do the other things, not because they are easy, but because they are hard; because that goal will serve to organize and measure the best of our energies and skills, because that challenge is one that we are willing to accept, one we are unwilling to postpone, and one we intend to win.

— John F. Kennedy, 1962

JFK's speech on going to the moon is one of the most inspiring ever made by a modern American president. The idea of choosing to do something not despite its difficulty, but precisely because it is difficult, captures the best of the American spirit.

That spirit Kennedy evoked has been with our nation from its birth. George Washington had to believe in achieving beyond what was seemingly possible, or he would have never agreed to lead an unprepared army against the greatest military the world had ever known.

As a coach who has led college tennis teams to national championships, I know that the qualities that make a leader are the same qualities required to develop athletes and championship teams. They include an inner drive to reach beyond one's grasp and to adapt and reinvent when the situation calls for it. They also include a focus on becoming the best you can be, rather than an obsession with results.

It all starts when individuals are willing to embrace uncertainty by moving out of their comfort zones. Unfortunately, from academics, to sports, to business, the world today is increasingly focused on comfort, brand management, and comparing favorably with others. That means people are not being pushed to move outside their comfort zones.

The answer to this problem can be found in competition—not the zero-sum, winner-take-all definition of competition, but the *true* meaning of competition: to strive together.

I've worked with analytical experts to develop a way to gauge the attributes that impact one's ability to strive together. I use it to help leaders build championship teams. Now, in this book, I am imparting that knowledge to anyone who is open to receiving it. It is imperative that future generations possess the attributes that support Strivership if they are to succeed in a world of rapid change and unprecedented challenges.

Do you want to build a company that others don't want to go up against because it's a struggle to keep up with your pace of innovation?

Do you want to coach a team that no one wants to face because your athletes execute relentlessly and respond to anything that opponents throw at them?

Do you want to lead a school that doesn't have to boast, "We develop lifelong learners," because your school is actually producing them?

If you're a business leader, educator, sports coach, or someone who has to or wants to lead in any capacity, this book is for you. I hope it provides you with some insights and inspires you to empower your people. The best leaders lead by allowing themselves to be led.

CHAPTER ONE

BIG SHOES TO FILL

If I have seen further it is by standing on the shoulders of giants.

—Isaac Newton

It was a midsummer morning in 1995 when my boss at the University of Texas—women's athletic director Jody Conradt—asked me to come to her office. This was just a couple of months after our women's tennis team had won its second NCAA title. The team had staged a miraculous comeback to upset number-one-seeded Florida in the finals. I had no idea why Jody wanted to meet, but I knew it would be interesting.

Jody understood what coaches go through. She was one of us. In addition to serving as the athletic director, she was also the coach of our women's basketball team. She was a living legend, well on her way to becoming one of the winningest coaches in the history of college basketball.

When I got to Jody's office, she had one question for me: "How did you do that?"

I was very flattered, but also caught off guard, so I blurted out the first thing that came to mind: "I didn't do it; the players did."

I immediately thought to myself, "That's a dumb thing to say. Maybe even flippant." Why couldn't I have come up with some clever response about the genius behind my team's great run?

On the surface, my answer to Jody's question may seem simplistic, but when I reflected on it, I realized that my response described what true leaders do: lead by being led.

The seeds of this approach to leadership had been planted in me many years before by my father and my college coach. I remembered my dad saying to me, "When your team has achieved something special, you want your people to say, '*We* did this.'" And I can still almost hear my coach, Jim Verdieck, telling us before virtually every practice, "Every day is a day to get better!"

These two people were my mentors.

Lessons on Leadership from My Father

My father, Bert Moore, was born in Sea Cliff, Long Island, New York. He later moved to Winchester, a suburb of Boston, where he played basketball and baseball for Winchester High School, and where he was elected president of the student body as a senior. After graduation, he attended Bowdoin College, where he was a point guard on the basketball team, a pitcher on the baseball team, and president of his fraternity. He also played a significant role in breaking down racial barriers that existed on college campuses.

My father attended school in the late 1940s, when fraternities were not exclusive organizations for privileged students, as they are known today. Back then, most students lived in and ate their meals at fraternity houses. They were an integral component of student life on campus—unless you were black. Due to the segregationist policies of the time, African American students were prohibited from joining fraternities. One of my dad's basketball teammates, Matt Branche, was an African American who was refused acceptance into my dad's fraternity. Believing this to be an injustice, my father led the effort to hire a lawyer, and he rallied key members of his fraternity's leadership team to travel to New York City, where they lodged a protest with the National Interfraternity Council. Their appeal to have Matt admitted to their fraternity was rejected, but that wasn't the end of it for these students. The fraternity leaders responded by pulling out of the national organization, thus becoming an independent fraternity. Then the fraternity admitted Matt and became one of the first integrated fraternities in the nation. When I learned of the story many years later, it struck me as an act of moral fortitude that left a lasting impression.

Upon graduating from Bowdoin, my father decided he wanted to become an educator. He took his first job at the Berkshire School in Western Massachusetts, where he taught history and coached varsity basketball. He then moved on to Belmont Hill School, where he became the director of development at the tender age of twenty-eight. But my dad's true desire was to run a school. After two years in his position at Belmont Hill, he applied for the position as head of the Tilton School in New Hampshire.

My dad was an underdog candidate. He was only thirty-one at the time. He wasn't concerned about his lack of experience, but was worried that his youthful appearance might hurt his chances. He decided to wear a fedora to the interview so he would look older. He was not accustomed to wearing hats, so when he got out of his car to greet the head of the search committee, his hat hit the top of the door and fell off. He was embarrassed by this Charlie Chaplin move, but recovered enough to do well in the interview and land the job.

Dad was fired up. Tilton had fallen on hard times, and he was excited to pump new life into the school. He was going to turn things around. But first he had to shake things up. In his first address to faculty and staff, he laid out a detailed plan for what he hoped to accomplish as head of school. He fervently put forth his plan to revive the school and lead it to a place of prominence.

He was met with silence and stares. Dad was shocked and angry. As my mother would later recall, he stormed into our home, venting, "How could they not see the brilliance of my plan!" As she tells it, he pounded his fist on the table and proclaimed, "I'm going to rule by edict!" I was six at the time and it was midafternoon, so I was probably on one of the school's vacant fields playing baseball with my buddies. I had missed my first lesson on how *not* to be a leader!

Dad soon learned that "ruling by edict" was managing, not leading. Like all leaders, he learned that to gain influence he must actually cede control. He began to empower his people in the decision-making process. Eventually the school was revitalized. Enrollment increased, new buildings and facilities were built, and several bright, young teachers were brought into the fold. Today, Tilton School has a dormitory named in Dad's honor: Moore Hall.

My father never was content with the status quo. He never believed in simply aligning with best practices. He sought out good ideas from his peers in education and from other seemingly disparate sources like the corporate world. He would use these ideas to help shape his own "best practices." I remember him saying over and over again, "The higher the standard, the higher the achievement."

My dad's work at Tilton began to catch the attention of boards of trustees at other schools around the country. After five or six years at Tilton, he started to look for a new challenge. He began flying around the country with my mom to interview for head-of-school openings. The place that caught his eye was not a big name school. It was Holland Hall, a small school with big ambitions in Tulsa, Oklahoma. The board wanted to build a new campus and thought my father was the right person to lead the effort.

To our friends and family, you would have thought we were going to load up a covered wagon and begin a long journey to the frontier. In the '60s, the Northeast was the center of the independent school universe—or at least that was the way it was portrayed. It was unheard of to move away from that—much less all the way to Oklahoma! The famous March 29, 1976, cover of the *New Yorker* illustrates a northeasterner's distorted view of the country perfectly: the area surrounding New York City's Ninth Avenue is outsized, while everything west of the Hudson River—the hinterlands—is portrayed as a sliver.

My dad was not interested in a prestigious East Coast prep school. He didn't want to be stuck presiding over an already established school dominated by well-heeled alums clinging to entrenched traditions. He was a builder and a forward thinker, and he realized that he would have to move away from this hidebound culture to develop the kind of school he wanted to lead, one that honored diverse and progressive thinking. He was impressed with Tulsa's growing economy, and the commitment of the school's board of trustees, so he accepted the offer and we moved to Oklahoma.

But once again Dad's youthful enthusiasm (he was still only thirty-seven) got him in trouble. He was convinced that Holland Hall needed a lot more than revitalizing. The school's board members were committed to his vision in principle, but they were not educators, so they did not realize how it would play out. Construction of a new campus would not begin for another four years. In the meantime, my dad came to believe that the school's culture needed a complete overhaul. Holland Hall was only fifteen years old, so its culture really hadn't had a chance to become entrenched. Most of the students were from affluent white families. The oil boom in Oklahoma and Texas had made many people wealthy beyond their dreams. Dad wanted to integrate African American students into this environment. But he understood that, to do so, he first had to change the culture.

He convinced the board of trustees to create more financial aid funds and then he enlisted teachers, coaches, and even parents to identify prospective students from middle-class white families. By diversifying the school with more middle-class students, he was able to change the cultural makeup of the school and set the table for integration. He thought that creating socioeconomic diversity among the white student population should be a first step.

My father started working right away through various networks to recruit excellent students from middle-class neighborhoods. This infusion transformed Holland Hall into a place with real spirit. Two of the new students who were part of this infusion went on to become the top students in my graduating class, four years later. The valedictorian was the first person in his family to go to college, and went on to become a pioneer in software development. The salutatorian, the son of a teacher in a local public school, is now a top official at the National Weather Service.

But change can be difficult. The influx of students from different environments in year one, along with rising expectations for teacher performance, caused an uproar. The board gave Dad one more year to "make things right." My father was undeterred. Despite being on the hot seat, he decided to go ahead and integrate the school in year two!

Interestingly, my father decided that the first African American student could not be a star athlete. When he was asked why not, he said that recruiting an athlete would put a label on the student, and people would assume that the student had only been allowed into the school for his athletic abilities. As such, the first African American student was the son of a custodian from a local public school. He was the first person in his family to go to college, and he went on to become an award-winning journalist, investigative reporter, and news anchor.

Eventually, a fresh new spirit evolved at the school. Dad was able to devote more time and energy to the construction of the new campus. He wanted the design and feel of the campus to facilitate and support a vibrant school community. In particular, he wanted school life to revolve around a huge commons area in the middle of the main building—a place where students could meet en masse every morning, as well as for impromptu and organized activities throughout the day. The commons area was two-tiered, with classrooms wrapped around the balcony above. He also introduced modular scheduling, and even went to England to study how schools were designed there.

Once the new campus was built, Dad got the itch to move on to another new challenge. It was then that he moved the family to Denver, where he successfully oversaw the merging of the Kent School for Girls and Denver Country Day School for Boys into what is known today as the Kent Denver School.

Eventually Dad moved on to Bloomfield Hills, Michigan, where he became director of the Cranbrook Schools, one of the most prestigious independent schools in the country. The school was dominated by the children of wealthy automobile industry executives. It was not unusual to walk into my parents' home on campus and see people like the CEO of General Motors sitting in the living room.

Dad would have been wise to take a page from his younger self. This was exactly the kind of environment he had avoided earlier in his career. He was presiding over a deeply entrenched school culture—shaking hands, kissing babies, and toeing the company line. Not surprisingly, he decided to leave after only three years.

I was a teacher and coach at Kent Denver for three years in the middle of Dad's tenure there. This afforded me the opportunity to watch him operate as part of his faculty. I was working in a different part of campus, but was able to watch him speak at full school gatherings, and occasionally was able to sit in on meetings that he conducted. At Kent Denver, he made sure to surround himself with really smart, accomplished people, just as he had at his other schools. It was fascinating to watch him go around the room in meetings, asking questions about problems they were trying to solve, even though he often already knew the answer. Like most leaders, he had a vision for the future and he articulated clear, long-term goals. What set him apart was that he did not assume that he knew exactly how to reach those goals. He did not seek to control the process. Dad trusted his people, and sought to empower each of them to contribute in their own unique way. "When my people have achieved something special, I want them to say, '*We* did this,'" he said. That was a crucial lesson for me that did not fully take hold until the middle of my coaching career.

Lessons from My Coach

My father was not my only source of inspiration. I would find another mentor in an unlikely place.

Growing up, I played football, basketball, and baseball, but I never had an interest in tennis until the summer before my senior year of high school. My parents had joined a local tennis club and taken up the game for recreation. I would take advantage of the club's pool to cool off after a day working construction at my summer job, or immediately following a baseball game. I was a pitcher with a live arm. I could throw hard. Unfortunately, I couldn't always control where the pitch went.

One night, following a particularly frustrating game, I borrowed a racket and started taking out my frustrations on the backboard instead of heading to the pool. The tennis director walked by and commented that I hit a nice ball and had potential. He offered to give me free lessons. In the late '60s and early '70s, before the tennis boom, our best athletes were not playing tennis. I was much bigger, stronger, and faster than most tennis players at the time. The tennis director kept emphasizing the advantage this gave me.

After a couple of months of lessons and practice, I decided to challenge Paul Lockwood, the number-one player on our high school team—who happened to also be ranked in the top twenty nationally. I figured that I could overpower him and certainly run down any shot he sent my way. *And run I did!* We played one set. I won only one game, and I was exhausted. But I received the most important tennis lesson of my life. Paul had extraordinary hands and the best touch of any player I've ever seen. He made me visit every part of the court multiple times. I gained a new level of respect for the game that day, and realized how much catching up I had to do.

I had vastly overrated the importance of strength and speed in the sport of tennis. I quickly realized that becoming an elite player is more difficult in tennis than any other sport. One of my former players at the University of Texas, Kelly Pace, was an All-American and made it into the top 150 in the world on the pro circuit. These accomplishments followed years of practice and matches, starting at a very young age. Kelly was also a good recreational golfer, playing occasionally when she needed a break from tennis. When she retired from the pro circuit in her early thirties, she decided to dedicate herself to golf. Within two years, she began playing tournaments. To date, she has finished ahead of five LPGA tour veterans in tournament play. Any athlete attempting to transition from another sport and master tennis in this same time frame would not be able to make the starting lineup on most Division III college teams, much less compete on the pro circuit.

It's amazing how many times I have witnessed better athletes lose to superior ball strikers on the recruiting trail. Paul did not outhit me that day; he made me suffer. Although I didn't realize it at the time, this experience was my first introduction to the true meaning of competition.

After I graduated from high school, I went to Knox College to play football and tennis. After my first year, I gave up football to concentrate on tennis. Unfortunately, the tennis program was not strong. More importantly, the team was coached by one of the football assistants, who had no background in tennis. I needed help with my game, so I started looking at other schools. I discovered the University of Redlands in California. Redlands had recently started an intriguing experimental college as part of its community, and it caught my eye. The school also had an extraordinarily successful tennis program led by a legendary coach named Jim Verdieck.

Coach Verdieck's program had already won small-college national championships, and he would go on to become the winningest coach in college tennis history. Looking back on his life, it is no surprise that he was able to reach stratospheric heights as a coach. His life experiences were extraordinary, even for a member of the Greatest Generation.

Coach Verdieck, who grew up in the blue-collar town of Colton, California, starred in multiple high school sports. When he graduated from high school, he enrolled in nearby San Bernardino Junior College and played football. His team lost only one game during his career, to Pasadena City College. Pasadena's star player was the legendary Jackie Robinson.

After graduating from San Bernardino Junior College, Jim was recruited by Stanford to play both football and baseball. He was part of the great Stanford football team called the "Wow Boys." Coached by Clark Shaughnessy, father of the T formation, the group featured Hall of Fame quarterback Frankie Albert. As a senior in 1940, he played on Stanford's national championship team, secured with a victory over Nebraska in the Rose Bowl.

After graduation, Coach V., like so many others from the Greatest Generation, enlisted in the armed services to fight in World War II. He served as a Marine Corps transport pilot and flew into danger many times. He also became the Marine Corps Fitness Champion! *The Stanford Daily* chronicled his most perilous mission:

> Marine Captain James A. Verdieck, Stanford graduate, hit the high spot of his Pacific assignments when he was ordered to ferry vital supplies to Iwo Jima. Captain Verdieck landed on the island on D-day, dropping parapacks of mail, food, and plasma, and removing wounded men. He

returned to the 'hell' from a base in the Marianas two days later to drop more vital cargoes.[1]

For his bravery during this famous World War II battle, Coach Verdieck was awarded the Distinguished Flying Cross.

Following the war, Verdieck was hired at Redlands to coach football and tennis. After several successful seasons as football coach, he decided to concentrate on tennis. He went on to record 921 wins. His teams won fifteen small-college national championships.

I was drawn more to Coach Verdieck's approach to coaching than his record of accomplishments. Though his record was extremely impressive, what set Coach V. apart was how he went about producing championship teams. Many tennis coaches recruit highly ranked players from the junior ranks who are viewed as close-to-finished products. Coach V. recruited talented players who were behind in their development and had fire in their belly. They were hungry to improve. His mantra was, "Every day is a day to get better."

Coach V. was a student of the game. He had decided to give up coaching football and focus on coaching tennis, which he had never played at a high level, but his background as a football and baseball athlete gave him a distinct advantage.

Many tennis coaches design practices as if they are conducting "group lessons," operating off the club pro model. Players are put through drills featuring seemingly endless reps of one stroke or a pattern of strokes. Coach V.'s practices focused on quality over quantity. He wanted his players to learn how to *use* their strokes. As a former football and baseball athlete, he understood that ability to execute at a high level under pressure is what separated champions

---

1   *The Stanford Daily* 107, no. 76, May 21, 1945.

from everyone else. Most of his rivals were developing players; Coach Verdieck was developing competitors.

Coach Verdieck was light-years ahead of his time. At times, the University of Redlands court complex seemed like a classroom for aspiring young coaches. After graduating, I would take a legal pad, sit in the stands, and watch him work. Dennis Van Der Meer, one of the most respected tennis clinicians in the history of the game, was among the many in his field who sought Coach Verdieck's counsel. Sometimes in the middle of practice, a phone that was mounted on the outside of an adjacent building would ring. It would be Dennis calling from overseas with a question about technique or tactics.

Dennis was the first tennis clinician to conduct programs to train coaches. He ran clinics all over the world. He also coached Margaret Court, the top player in the world at the time. The year after I graduated, he staged one of his clinics at the Redlands court complex and brought her along. During lunch hour each day, he trained her on court one. I could not afford the clinic, but I made sure to be in the stands with my legal pad every day at lunch hour!

Coach Verdieck passed away in 2004. His memorial service at the University of Redlands chapel was attended by several tennis luminaries. After the service, I joined some of them, including Dennis Van Der Meer, on a stroll over to the courts. We were recounting great stories about Coach. At one point I asked Dennis with a smile, "Coach once told me that he taught you 90 percent of what you know. Is that true?" Dennis responded, "That's about right."

Then, as if on cue, a few of us, Dennis included, reached into our coat pockets and pulled out handwritten notes we'd received from Coach V. I had received mine after a clinic I had conducted at a coaches' conference on Hilton Head Island a couple of years before. Three hundred coaches were in attendance, sitting in the bleachers in front of me. Just as I was about to start, I saw someone out of the corner of my eye bringing a folding chair onto the court behind me. It was Coach Verdieck, sitting all by himself, ready to critique me. Talk about nervous! His note provided feedback on my performance that began with a brief compliment before posing some very challenging questions. All of us had received handwritten letters at some point that offered the same kind of critique. It was classic Coach Verdieck. I loved it!

I didn't have a clue what I wanted to do after graduation, so I cobbled together jobs providing tennis lessons and working in admissions for Johnston College. One day, I was approached by two students who wanted the University of Redlands to start a women's basketball team. Title IX legislation had passed and they had taken their case to the athletic director, who had approved the formation of a team. They asked me if I would be willing to coach the team. I accepted the opportunity, and became the first women's basketball coach at the University of Redlands. To this day, I don't know why they asked me to be the coach. I had played high school basketball, but had never coached anything before.

We won one game in my first year. Our opponents' average winning margin was astronomical. The team consisted entirely of current students, some of whom had not even played high school basketball. On top of that, I was terrible! I learned many valuable lessons that first year, the most important being the difference between being a player and being a coach. It looks a lot different on the other side. With the help of some new recruits, our record improved in my second year. We even pushed Division I Pepperdine to the brink, losing on a half-court shot at the buzzer.

After my first year as basketball coach, the coaching position for women's tennis became open. I applied, got the position, and coached both sports for a year. We started the tennis season by losing eight to one to Cal Poly Pomona, the previous year's conference champion. This disappointing start did not deter me. I channeled Coach Verdieck's mantra: "Every day is a day to get better." We had great team practices, and I made sure to work one-on-one and in small groups with the players outside of regular practice. The team made tremendous strides in just a few months. At the season-ending conference tournament, we again faced Cal Poly, this time in the semis. We won five to four. The next day, we upset Pepperdine to win the conference championship. It was really special for the players, all of whom were walk-ons, since Division III schools do not give athletic scholarships. They had put in long hours with the goal of seeing just how much they could improve. It was a very rewarding experience. Thanks to the values Coach Verdieck had instilled in me, I had my first taste of what it was like to be part of a championship team.

Coach Verdieck was old school in many ways. He coached at a time when athletes did what they were told. You did not question the coach. Athletes almost never asked, "Why?" For better or worse, this is just the way it was. And parents supported coaches. I would never have considered complaining about coaches to my parents. They would have responded by essentially saying "deal with it." Furthermore, if a coach told my parents that I was not working hard enough, I would be the one in trouble.

This put a lot of power in the coach's hands, and many coaches abused it. Great coaches, like great leaders in every industry, demonstrate two central qualities: strong ego drive and empathy. Coaches who have empathy but lack a strong ego drive do not last very long because they are unable to provide a strong sense of where the ship is heading. Coaches who demonstrate strong ego drive but not empathy can be successful in spurts, but they wear out their welcome quickly.

Coach Verdieck had both a strong ego and empathy. He knew what he wanted and was very direct about it, but it was never personal. He never fell into the trap of attempting to be fair. He treated everyone equally. He demonstrated empathy by putting himself in the shoes of each of his players, so when he told you what to do, it was typically in line with what was right for you. But you definitely had to earn his respect.

Our relationship obviously changed when I became the women's coach. I remember one instance when he was using all the courts for his practice, despite the fact that I had reserved four of them for my women's team. Instead of deferring to him, I yelled to him from four courts away, "Coach, we have four of these courts reserved now for practice." I started trembling as he slowly walked over to me. I showed him the reservation sheet. He looked me in the eye and said, "You're right," then removed his players from those courts. This man was a living legend. In hindsight, it's hard to believe I objected to him so freely. Back then, your coaches, your bosses, and your elders were authoritarian figures. But the really good ones respected you when you stood up to them and you were in the right. It was a moment that truly endeared him to me, and helped me grow as a person.

Applying Those Lessons

I left the University of Redlands the following year because, at the time, it was not possible to build a career as a college coach unless you were willing to teach physical education. Unsure of what to do, I settled on following in my father's footsteps. I applied for teaching positions at several private schools. My applications were too late, so I was forced to move back to Colorado, where I taught at a club in Denver for the summer. Suddenly, an opportunity appeared.

Someone at the club told me the University of Colorado was looking for a women's tennis coach. I applied and got the job.

I coached the Colorado women's team while also teaching and coaching part time at Kent Denver to make ends meet. After four years, the men's coaching job opened, and I was offered the opportunity to coach both teams. I jumped at the opportunity for two reasons: I would get to do even more of what I loved to do, and I could quit teaching and devote myself to coaching full time.

My career as a coach was now full steam ahead. I would not be distracted by the duties of a second job; I could focus entirely on building a competitive team. I was way too young to be a head coach at a Division I school, much less coaching two teams at a time, but it didn't faze me. I was in my twenties, an age of innocence, when you don't know what you don't know, and everything is possible. In my fourth year, the women's team cracked the top twenty-five nationally. It was a great accomplishment, but the overconfidence that resulted from this early success would come back to bite me.

I had no inclination that I would end up at a place like the University of Texas, where expectations would be inconceivably high and where I would face the first true test of my abilities. I would confront challenges there that forced me to sink or swim. At that moment, the lessons that I had learned from the two mentors in my life would serve as a guide as I made the transition from a young, hyperenthusiastic upstart to a leader.

A lot of pain and suffering goes into becoming a successful leader. You cannot become a leader through training; there is no formula; leading is an art. It

> *You cannot become a leader through training; there is no formula; leading is an art. It must be cultivated over time.*

must be cultivated over time. My dad's admonition, "Lead by being led," and Coach Verdieck's mantra, "Every day is a day to get better," provided me with a foundational understanding of what it means to become a leader. It really started coming together for me when I examined the essence of competition. This was the nexus of the concept of Strivership, my Striver Quotient® Assessment Tool, and the beginning of what would become Moore Leadership.

While it is important to understand what this book offers, it is crucial to understand what it does not. Unlike most books written in the leadership genre, this one will not provide you with a formula.

Formulas are prescriptive. They are designed to provide a quick fix at a time when we've become results-obsessed as a society. The bar for achievement in our country has never been so low. Any result will do. My dad used to say, "The higher the standard, the higher the achievement." Now we've defaulted to just "get a win." We no longer dream about achievements that seem unimaginable. Success must always be within our grasp—whatever it takes to embellish our personal brands. We have lost the motivation to stretch ourselves at a time when solutions to the complex problems we face require us to reach beyond our grasp.

In this book, I will provide you with a framework for what it takes to build a championship team in business and in sports.

This book is about replacing "built to last," a mantra for the Industrial Age, when change was incremental, with "built to invent, adapt, and reinvent," a mantra for the world of rapid change that we now live in. In business, in sports, and in schools, leaders must once again challenge their people to stretch beyond their perceived limitations in pursuit of goals that seem out of reach.

In past generations, most problems had solutions, and you could almost always find established methods to solve them. Old-fashioned hard work and grit sufficed. In today's world of rapid change, many of the problems we encounter require unconventional problem-solving abilities. This requires all hands on deck. Leaders must lead by being led.

CHAPTER TWO

THE TRUE MEANING OF COMPETITION

The credit belongs to the [person] who is actually in the arena, whose face is marred by dust and sweat and blood; who strives valiantly; who errs, who comes short again and again, because there is no effort without error and shortcoming ...

—Theodore Roosevelt

I like to surround myself with people who are smarter than I am and think differently. My dad and Coach Verdieck were my mentors, and they certainly fit that description. When it comes to my peers, I engage the most with those who challenge my thinking. Geoff McDonald and Paul Wardlaw, both national championship coaches, have been there for me throughout my career as a coach. In education, Kevin Moore is a bright, young teacher who has provided me with keen, prescient insights. In my latest endeavors, it has been Jimmy Treybig, Tony Capasso, and Jim Albrecht who have counseled and advised me on issues relevant to the business world. All of these people have contributed mightily to the message I am about to impart.

It was a well-timed discussion with Paul Wardlaw that set in motion a novel perspective on building championship teams. I first met Paul at the Intercollegiate Tennis Association's Coaches Convention in the early '90s. At that time, he was coaching the women's team at Kenyon College, while I was doing the same job at the University of Texas. Paul was a very successful coach. His Kenyon teams had won three NCAA Division III national titles. I had the utmost respect for him because of the focus he placed on developing his players as people. That's what he does best: Paul develops people. He believes that if you helped the *person* grow, the *athlete* will naturally develop and eventually perform at a higher level.

Paul's mind is always churning. He is a thinker with an uncanny ability to distill a complex issue down to a few key questions that switch on a light bulb in your head. I always take something valuable away from our conversations.

In the summer of 2007, we had a phone conversation that really lit some bulbs in my head. I was retired from coaching and had accepted a position as athletics director at Trinity Episcopal School in Austin. Paul and I were discussing the challenges of working with young people and their parents. We both agreed something had changed as the millennial generation arrived on campus. Parents seemed to respond to their children's participation in athletics differently. A willingness to allow their children to grow and develop seemed to vanish, replaced by an almost manic daily obsession with ensuring that their children compared favorably with their peers. Parents no longer seemed concerned with what was best for their child's long-term development. It did not seem to occur to most of these parents that someday, their children would have to spread their own wings. Making the varsity team, getting into a prestigious college, or attracting a college scholarship offer took precedence over the long view. It seemed to us that all of the focus was being placed on external motivators, stunting the growth and development of a strong sense of self.

"Why do so many parents seem intent on making sure their kids compare favorably with their peers?" I asked Paul. "Why are they so afraid to leave them alone and allow them to compete? It seems like 'compete' is a dirty word now."

Paul replied by asking me if I knew the origin of the word *compete*.

The word comes from the Latin word *competere*, which has two root words: *com* and *petere*. Com means "together," like community, and petere means "to strive." Taken together, the original meaning of compete is "strive together."

Our society has lost sight of what it means to compete. *Striving together* is the essence of true competition. When two people compete, there is usually tension, but ultimately, regardless of the outcome, true competitors view competition as something that makes them better. At its essence, competition is not personal, because you are always, first and foremost, competing to a standard. Competing is about striving together; it's a shared purpose.

> At its essence, competition is not personal, because you are always, first and foremost, competing to a standard. Competing is about striving together; it's a shared purpose.

Unfortunately, what competing now means to many parents is far removed from the true essence of the word, particularly at the middle school and high school levels. The modern definition of compete, "to outdo another for prize or supremacy," is a clear indication of how distorted the meaning has become. Competing is now viewed strictly as a zero-sum endeavor. In the end, there is a winner and a loser—that's it.

Once I came to understand this, I could see why, in the current climate, parents so carefully select times when their children are vulnerable to competition. The objective is to ensure that one child's talents are showcased in a way that allows him or her to compare favorably to other children. This perspective has led to the enormous rise of outside sports and a steady, gradual devaluation of middle school and high school sports. During the latter part of my career at Texas, I was recruiting athletes in this environment. Sadly, too many of them arrived on campus as branded commodities with no true sense of self.

After retiring, I was able to get a firsthand look at what was happening in the youth sports ecosystem. I coached high school boys' basketball as well as a seventeen-and-under AAU boys' team that traveled the country to recruiting showcase tournaments. Coaching the high school team was one of the most rewarding experiences of my coaching career. The athletes steadily improved as individuals, while playing for something bigger than themselves—their school. The boys on the AAU team played strictly for themselves, because outside sports are about getting exposure to and showcasing your talents for college coaches. Athletes would talk about the importance of playing a specific role to help the team win; that is, until doing so interfered with their ability to market themselves to college coaches. Outside sports teams are run by coaches who are themselves controlled by the parents. They are effectively client services providers. The parents pressure them to treat their children "fairly," which is often code for "everyone gets to showcase their talents."

Coaches at the middle school and high school levels also face parent pressure. There are precious few cases where the leader of the school has the coach's back, and the coach feels empowered to do what all great coaches do: treat the athletes equally. Unfortunately, there are even fewer leaders in college sports, which is ultimately a business, with administrators beholden to commercial interests. Instead of leading, they're pressured to simply manage the brand. They want to win, but only because it fuels the business plan. At the same time, they want the athletes—their customers—to be treated fairly, so they evaluate coaches on two criteria that are impossible to reconcile: "What was your team's record this season?" and "Did your athletes have a 'positive' experience?"

If a coach's goal is to treat each athlete *fairly*, the team's performance becomes a lesser priority. Everyone on the basketball team gets a chance to shoot, even the players who shoot poorly. When the goal is to treat each athlete *equally*, the team comes first. If you are a poor shooter, you must find other ways to help the team win. If you would like to become a better shooter, you put in the hours outside of practice to improve your shot. This is exactly the mind-set that young people encounter when they enter the real world. They are not always afforded the opportunity to try the job of their choosing. Unfortunately, before entering the real world, young people are conditioned to compare, not to compete.

The same thing is happening on the academic side. Seventy-five percent of the grades given in college are As and Bs. Forty-five percent are As, which is now the most common grade. At some universities, when students are not happy with their grade on a test, they are allowed to retake it. The goal is the same in both academics and athletics: ensure that the customers are satisfied.[2]

As I prepared for my first year at Trinity, I questioned how this disconnected reality ever gained traction. Then it clicked. I recalled a moment in the midseventies, when I was a teacher and coach at the Kent Denver School in Englewood, Colorado. One day, at the conclusion of a middle school faculty meeting, the director asked if there was any new business. The assistant director said, "Yes. I think we should discuss deemphasizing competition. I feel that it's important to make sure every child feels special."

"Whoa!" I thought to myself. "What's wrong with competition? And what does 'make sure every child feels special' mean?"

I was in my early twenties and just starting out, so I had no frame of reference. But based on my past experience as a student and athlete, these ideas were foreign to me. I certainly couldn't recall any of my teachers and coaches being overly concerned about whether I felt "special." Sure, competition can certainly be over the top at times, but what doesn't kill you makes you stronger.

While recalling this "aha!" moment at Kent Denver, I realized that the "every child should be made to feel special" mind-set had been brewing in our culture for some time. My colleague's comments at Kent Denver reflected the kinds of discussions that had already been sparked by what came to be known as the self-esteem movement.

The self-esteem movement was fueled in part by books like *How to Raise Your Self-Esteem,* by Nathaniel Branden. In his book, Branden spends an entire chapter stressing a key component of building strong self-esteem: learning to take responsibility for one's

---

2   Tom Lindsay, "The 'Other' College Scandal: Grade Inflation Has Turned Transcripts into Monopoly Money," *Forbes*, March 30, 2019, https://www.forbes.com/sites/tomlindsay/2019/03/30/the-other-college-scandal-grade-inflation-has-turned-transcripts-into-monopoly-money/#4328304f4182.

own actions. Gradually, that crucial part of the message faded. As the movement gained steam, adults took an increasing amount of control over their children's lives, robbing young people of the chance to learn about the importance of owning their actions. Even the government got involved in the hype. In 1988, the California state government passed legislation that mandated the teaching of self-esteem. Expectations for self-accountability on the part of young people faded from the self-esteem lexicon. I had seen this shift during the latter part of my coaching career at Texas. Instead of "What can *I* do to get better," athletes started most conversations with something like, "Why aren't *you* more positive with us?"

I had been a student and an athlete before the advent of the self-esteem movement, and a teacher and coach as it evolved and gained a foothold in our society. I had lived through the paradigm shift. I certainly did not want to go back to the pre-self-esteem movement approach to athletics. The problem with coaches in past generations was that "my way or the highway" was the modus operandi. It was a "what doesn't kill you makes you stronger" mentality—survival of the fittest. There were certainly athletes who came out of that kind of experience stronger in the end. Competition for those young people could be viewed as "striving together" because it did make them better. But this old-school approach scarred too many young people at the middle school and high school level who were behind in their emotional and/or physical development. If young athletes were too far behind, they would be weeded out.

Time for a New Direction

It became clear to me that a fresh perspective on competing was desperately needed. The conversation with Paul Wardlaw had inspired me to look back and trace how we had moved from the old-school approach to athletics to the current mentality. In past generations, competition had been taken too seriously and a course correction was definitely needed. Unfortunately, we had made a 360-degree adjustment instead of the 180 degrees that were in order. As the self-esteem movement gained traction, we moved from "what doesn't kill you makes you stronger" to "ensuring that you are made to feel special." Neither of these mantras serves the true meaning and purpose of competition.

One common thread throughout it all is that adults have remained in charge. In past generations, coaches had the power and operated in a top-down manner. If the coach was upset with your son or daughter, you punished your child. Now coaches are viewed as client service providers by the parents, who have wrestled power from them.

I felt a sense of urgency to influence the transition from an approach to athletics centered on what adults want to an approach that empowered young people to take control of their own performance. The timing was especially urgent because of the need to prepare young people for the increasingly disruptive, unstable world they would enter upon finishing school. As such, I decided to develop a philosophy of athletics for Trinity Episcopal based on the true meaning of competition. I began the process by drastically shortening and simplifying our athletics handbook, in large part to place primary focus on purpose, not mission. Our purpose would be empowering our young athletes to compete in athletics in a way that would help prepare them to compete in their first truly big game: day one of job one.

Competition in sports is about striving together in key relationships to Self, to Team, and to Coach. On day one of their first jobs, young people are confronted with very similar relationships. I wanted our athletes to focus on building these three relationships independently of their parents. I outlined policies that would empower them to do so.

Two of the policies were real paradigm-shifters for most twenty-first-century parents: parents were not allowed to communicate with a coach until their child had done so, and parents were not allowed to attend practices. There was a time when parents didn't come to school unless required to do so. Now, at most schools, you can't turn around without running into one.

Instead of taking a conventional approach to messaging by giving speeches and issuing white papers, I decided to cultivate these new concepts through my interactions with parents. I made a point of going to as many athletic events as possible, engaging with parents. I also wrote a blog for Trinity parents, "Youth Sports Sanity," that appeared on the school website. I tackled difficult topics by focusing on stories about elite athletes and highly successful coaches. Through both the blog and my interactions with parents, I sought to reinforce the importance of viewing the development of competitive relationships to Self, Team, and Coach through the lens of striving together, not the modern zero-sum view of competing.

Developing a competitive *Relationship to Self* involves understanding that if you want to improve, you are going to have to compete with yourself. If you want to make yourself better, you're going to have to change, and change is difficult. As such, you are your number-one obstacle when it comes to changing. Pushing yourself to change will undoubtedly make you uncomfortable, and being uncomfortable is a state of vulnerability that most of us are conditioned to avoid. When you venture outside of your comfort zone, you are confronted with problems you have not faced before.

Often, attempting to solve these problems will require you to learn a new set of skills. Building those new skills will take time, and you can't be sure how much time. What is important is to commit to the process, not some expedited result. Making changes can hurt your performance in the short term, so you will be challenged to embrace failure (and possible embarrassment) and learn from setbacks.

Venturing into uncharted territory makes you vulnerable, which causes you to project a more authentic self. A strong Relationship to Self is crucial, but it's not enough. Most of the work done in the real world today is done in teams.

Relationship to Team is inextricably linked to Relationship to Self because building a competitive relationship to your team also requires you to move out of your comfort zone. Developing a competitive Relationship to Team requires understanding that if the team is going to succeed, each team member must accept his or her role. However, this does not mean *blending in*—a term many coaches use that frustrates me. Great teams do not consist of people who simply *fit*. They are full of people who *stand out* in their roles. Striving together as a team requires a commitment by team members to push one another while simultaneously allowing themselves to be open to being pushed. At the same time, team members must be committed to supporting each other, even teammates with whom they might have a personality conflict. On great teams, what happens in the locker room stays in the locker room. Good teammates support each other to all outside entities unconditionally at all times. However, internal support cannot be unconditional. If you have a serious issue with a teammate that is compromising your ability to offer support, you must communicate with that teammate openly and in a timely manner.

If you are not pushing your teammates and communicating with them, you are not truly supporting them. Respect is the first priority of a team. Think about it: if we were on the battlefield in some far-off land together, what would be more important: that you like me as an individual, or that you respect my abilities? It is respect that's really important on a team, and people tend to like each other more once respect is established. As members of the same team, you share a common goal. Respectfully challenging a teammate is not personal; it's calling on them to honor their end of the relationship. Everyone becomes uncomfortable, but embracing this discomfort strengthens relationships among teammates.

Developing a competitive *Relationship to Coach/Boss* is inextricably linked to Relationship to Self as well. Striving together with your coach/boss also requires you to move out of your comfort zone. This relationship is very similar to Relationship to Team, except for one major difference: in sports, it is crucial for athletes to respect that coaches know what they are doing. In past generations, coaches were respected, sometimes even revered. If the coach indicated that Johnny wasn't working hard enough, Johnny would get a whuppin'. Today, the coach is the one who suffers a (veritable) whuppin'.

Parents no longer take the long view. It's not about helping their children develop into young adults, capable of spreading their own wings. Parents now expect coaches to serve as copilots. Parents' missions are to ensure their children will compare favorably to their peers, and to shoot down anything that might make them uncomfortable along the way. The better the protection, the better the chance of hauling in more trophies.

At Trinity, I sought to cultivate a new way of viewing an old-school approach to the Self and Team relationships. Relationship to Coach, however, needed a complete overhaul. I advocated for a completely new Relationship to Coach mind-set. I was not going to return to supporting the command and control approach, or succumb to the current coach-as-copilot mentality. The former style requires a strong ego, but lacks empathy. The latter mentality eventually hollows out any sense of strong internal drive. I wanted our coaches to be viewed as leaders, and real leaders possess both attributes.

I sought to cultivate in our young athletes a sense of respect, not reverence, for coaches. This respect starts with the belief that coaches can be trusted to know what is best. When and if a serious issue arises, whether it is a question like "Why are you having me try this new technique?" or a personal issue, it is the athlete's responsibility to communicate. The coach's responsibility is to ensure that the athlete is heard.

Running to Mom and Dad or any other third parties with a problem creates a distraction for athletes and their teammates. Athletes must trust and support their coaches unconditionally to everyone outside the team. Internally, they must communicate with the coaches—doing otherwise is not truly supporting them. Championship teams are made up of individuals who push themselves and one another. They are accountable to themselves and to each other.

Inevitably, my approach created waves. It caused a kind of systemic disruption that is virtually unheard of in schools. Education is the most change-averse field in existence. Surprisingly, a small group of people immediately adopted my approach, while another group was repulsed by it. Prominent school consultant Michael Thompson once advised school leaders that 20 percent of their students' parents would be adamantly against them no matter which course of action they chose. I would say that 20 percent proved to be about right in my case.

A classic example of the friction I encountered occurred when a parent marched into my office one day and said, "You don't understand. All this relationship stuff is great, but my son is going to get a scholarship." Anything short of making the A-team wouldn't cut it. When I was younger, this kind of encounter would have caused me to become defensive. By the time I got to Trinity, however, I was better at handling these situations. Instead of becoming defensive, I went on offense by responding, "If your child's long-term goal is to get a scholarship, what we're doing here becomes even more important." I would save more blunt responses for people like Lost Cause Dad, who told me that what we were doing would imperil his son's career.

A much larger group of parents may have been initially shocked by my approach, but later became intrigued by it. They realized that I was onto something, especially when I would ask them questions like, "Did your mom or dad come to your practices when you were in school?" This group of parents wanted to do the right thing, but also felt pressure to keep up with the Joneses. The most common example was Volleyball Mom, the type who would always complain to me about her child's coach. My standard reply was, "What a great opportunity and learning experience this is for your daughter. Someday she is probably going to have a bad boss. Has she communicated with her coach?" Despite the angst, Volleyball Mom typically stayed engaged with me. Some of the parents from Trinity remain in touch to this day.

At the very least, I was able to get parents thinking about the long view.

The Nexus of an Idea

During my time at Trinity Episcopal I was able to begin the process of fleshing out my coaching philosophy. I hadn't given my philosophy much thought before that point. When you coach a college sport, you are on all the time. You are completely immersed in what you are doing. There is not much time for reflection.

By my third year at Trinity, I had begun to expand my horizons. That's when I started "Youth Sports Sanity." With the help of Julia Smith, the school's director of communications, the blog became a hit, going viral within the school community and providing me with a forum to articulate my philosophy.

The more I thought about it, the more I came to believe that losing sight of the true meaning of competition had impacted every aspect of our modern world. People no longer viewed competition as a means to improve. That zero-sum, all-or-nothing perspective had become pervasive, reinforcing the notion that results were all that mattered. Now that I saw the problem, I was itching to find a new challenge; an opportunity to reintroduce the true meaning of competition on a bigger stage.

That kind of opportunity fell into my lap when Mike Davis, the head of school at Colorado Academy in Lakewood, Colorado, reached out to me about becoming the school's new director of athletics. We had several discussions over the phone before I travelled to Colorado for a series of interviews. It was Mike's second year at Colorado Academy and his first head job, despite the fact that he was only thirty-nine years old.

I was direct with him about my approach to athletics: "Mike, I am a troublemaker. I'm not a typical AD. I will push the envelope instead of leaning on go-to clichés like 'Our goal is to teach life lessons.' We will win more games in the process, but when our students return to campus years after graduating, winning will not be what they want to talk about. Our young people will learn how to compete, and this will prepare them for what is now a very different and extremely competitive real world. The scoreboard will take care of itself."

I had known Mike since his days in Austin as head of the upper school at St. Stephen's Episcopal School. He had been monitoring what I was doing at Trinity, and was well aware that I would bring an entirely different approach to athletics. Mike was looking for something different, and he had a reason other than winning in mind. He said, "I want your department to compete with the fine arts department, which is very strong here. I want all of our departments to strive for excellence!"

If I was going to continue working in education, then this was the perfect opportunity. I liked the people I met at Colorado Academy; the school had a great vibe. I was straightforward with all of the administrators, board members, and parents that I met. This was an opportunity to work for an inspiring young head of school who shared my vision. I would also have the opportunity to run a much larger program and go to-to-toe with archrival Kent Denver, the school that my dad had created, where I had taught many years before. Kent Denver had become a sports powerhouse, winning multiple state championships. Colorado Academy athletics had a lot of catching up to do, but I believed that cultivating excellence could help to close that gap.

Colorado Academy would have been the perfect job for me if I had decided to stay in education. However, the desire to make a broader impact dissuaded me from accepting the job. After much thought, I decided the best path for me was to start a leadership consulting business. I sensed that the timing was right to bring the true meaning of competition to an even wider audience. Leaders in organizations of all types were struggling to cope with a new and unstable real world characterized by rapid change. The disruptive twenty-first-century economy was a major driving factor of this instability. Product cycles had shortened drastically and there was constant pressure to create something new.

I came across an IBM study that asked 1,500 CEOs, "What is the biggest challenge you face?" Many business experts assumed the answer would be something obvious, like "better management discipline." Instead, the overwhelming majority of respondents reported that "coping with change" was their most pressing challenge. They went on to say that they were operating in a world that is increasingly volatile, uncertain, and complex.[3]

These respondents said something else that really caught my attention. The majority admitted that they felt ill-prepared to cope with this challenging new environment. I thought "coping" seemed like a weak response to the realities of this new rapidly changing world. These CEOs seemed to view the changes as threatening.

I wanted to help leaders view this environment through the lens of what is possible, instead of seeing only obstacles. I wanted to help them learn that embracing the discomfort would enable them to thrive in this environment of ambiguity, opening up all kinds of opportunities.

People in human resources often promote the idea of creating collaborative cultures to more effectively "cope" with these new realities. *Collaboration*, a word defined as "working together," was originally used to drive efficiency, not productivity. *To collaborate* has become an ever-ready, catch-all term suited more for the challenge

---

3   IBM, "Capitalizing on Complexity: Insights from the Global Chief Executive Officer Study," May 2010, https://www.ibm.com/downloads/cas/1VZV5X8J.

of planning for the company retreat than for solving difficult problems. This has become the typical response of my generation: to treat a serious challenge as a threat, not an opportunity. When baby boomers in leadership positions perceive a situation as threatening, the thought of not comparing favorably with the competition petrifies them. Instead of viewing it as an opportunity to compete, they turn to impression management to create the perception that they are winning. Whatever it takes to compare favorably with the competition.

I was not going to be that kind of boomer; I wanted to help leaders thrive in ambiguity. I had been confronted by a challenging, high-pressure environment at University of Texas, and chose to respond by competing, not comparing. It doesn't matter if it's business or sports; championship teams are not built by developing a collaborative culture. A commitment to simply work together is not enough.

A paradigm shift in the way that people viewed leadership was desperately needed. I would soon begin introducing a new paradigm to leaders in business, sports, and education in the form of Strivership.

CHAPTER THREE

THE POWER OF STRIVERSHIP

Some people see things that are and ask "Why?" I dream of things that never were and ask "Why not?"

—George Bernard Shaw

Strivership is an ethic of internal competition based on a shared commitment to strive together to achieve beyond all expectations. Championship teams embrace Strivership because they know that if they strive together they will be ready for anything the Competition throws at them.

However, most teams are doing exactly the opposite. They talk about things like "commitment to continuous improvement," but in reality they are focused on competing externally, not internally. The vast majority of business teams, sports teams, and schools put most of their effort into tracking what the Competition is doing and reacting to it. Obviously, a strategy-first approach can work to a degree because a lot of these teams become winning teams, at least in the short term. It takes courage to resist focusing on the Competition. It can be very tempting to follow the herd. After all, who wants to think they're being left behind?

But competing externally is a zero-sum endeavor. It involves engaging in obsessive benchmarking to gauge how we compare. A sense of utility, functionality, and robotic collaboration pervades. These teams have a culture, but no spirit. They talk about continuous improvement, but they don't live it. This limits what can be achieved.

If you are committed to Strivership, the results take care of themselves. The sky is the limit for championship teams because they are always reaching beyond their grasp. Questions like, "How do we compare?" rarely come up because everyone is thinking, "How good can we become?" Championship teams exude a Spirit of Strivership, a sense that everyone involved is excited about getting better together, every day. A commitment to continuous improvement requires change, and change is difficult. Team members must step outside their comfort zones and strive together in all of their relationships.

During my coaching career, I was fortunate to have several athletes who embodied Strivership. One of those athletes was Kelly Pace, the only player to start in the singles lineup for both of our NCAA Championship teams at University of Texas. In her first year at Texas, Kelly played number-three singles on a team that advanced to the finals of the NCAA Championships. As a sophomore, she played number-two singles on our first national championship team. With our top player graduating, she became the odds-on favorite to inherit the number-one singles position as a junior. Unfortunately, two unforeseen circumstances short-circuited that plan.

When Kelly committed to Texas at the beginning of her senior year of high school, she was five feet five inches tall. When she arrived for her first year, she was five feet nine inches. Boys have been known to experience growth spurts like that late in their high school years, but for girls, it is rare. As a junior player, Kelly made up for her lack of height with quickness; she ran down every ball. But she had difficulty generating power. After her growth spurt, she was much taller and longer-limbed. Unfortunately, this created a catch-22. Longer limbs enable a player to create more leverage and generate more power, but sudden growth spurts like Kelly experienced can weaken joints. Early in the fall of her junior year, Kelly, a right-hander, injured her left wrist, and the doctor told her that she would no longer be able to hit her two-hand backhand. She would have to rely on a one-hand backhand instead. This was a devastating blow to Kelly, because her backhand was her stronger side. Many people would have viewed this development as career-ending.

I saw a silver lining. I met with Kelly for lunch the day she received the doctor's news. After acknowledging that this was a tough setback, I said to her, "This is a great opportunity! You have been working on playing more aggressively by trying to develop your forehand as a weapon. Now you *have* to do this! Your two-hand backhand was your stronger side, but it was not a weapon. Now you have to use your one-hander to set up your forehand. To me, your future as a competitor is now even more promising than it was before."

My words lifted her spirits a bit because she knew I was not one to engage in hyperbole. This setback would negatively impact her progress in the short term, but with the right attitude, she could turn it into a positive in the long term. She got right to work, determined to use this obstacle to become an even better competitor.

The other obstacle blocking Kelly's ascendance to the top singles position was the arrival of a Czech player named Lucie Ludvigova, a transfer from Grand Canyon College. Lucie had traveled to the US after finishing high school to play professional tournaments as an amateur at the urging of her older brother, Jan Ludvig. Jan recognized the opportunities that existed for Lucie in the US. Several years earlier, he had pulled off a harrowing escape across the border into Austria from what was then Communist Czechoslovakia. He was forced to stay in an Austrian refugee camp for six months before he was able to make his way to the US, where he went on to play for the National Hockey League's New Jersey Devils.

Jan Ludvig was a tough guy, and so was his sister. In Communist Czechoslovakia, young people who had athletic potential were not allowed to choose their sport; the Czech government made that decision for them. Lucie was initially selected to join the national ski racing team before she was switched to track, where she ran some impressive eight hundred meter times. Finally, she was told she would be moved to tennis. She quickly developed into one of the top junior players in Czechoslovakia.

After playing in several pro tournaments during her trip to the US, Lucie decided that she wanted to play college tennis. She didn't speak a word of English, so her only option was junior college. She chose to attend Midland Junior College, where she played for one year. During that time, she not only learned English, but also earned stellar grades and won the National Junior College Singles Title. The following year, Midland dropped its tennis program, forcing Lucie to transfer. She chose Grand Canyon University because, in addition to having a strong tennis program, it was a Division II school, which meant she would have the option of transferring to a Division I school the next year without having to sit out a year. Lucie went undefeated in singles that year and won the National Division II singles title. The following year she became a Longhorn.

Like Kelly, Lucie was also a grinder; she sought to outlast people. You had to beat her; she was not going to beat herself. And she never took a point off. I thought both players could play at a much higher level by setting up points to use their forehand as a weapon. Put plainly, they had to learn to win more points outright by forcing errors instead of always waiting for opponents to crumble. It's tough to be consistently successful playing a game of attrition against top players. Lucie's advantage? She had already developed a strong one-hand backhand.

Immediately upon arriving at Texas, Lucie hit the ground running. In college tennis, team matches are played in the spring. Most coaches view individual tournaments in the fall as an opportunity to prepare for the spring, almost like an extension of practice. But to the players, individual results, particularly at prestigious events, are important. Lucie dominated the off-season during her first fall at Texas by nearly sweeping all three major college tournaments. She advanced to the finals of the Clay Court Championships, then won both the All-American and Indoor Championships.

Kelly did not fare as well that fall because developing her new aggressive tactics required a major paradigm shift. She began the fall by losing in the first round at the Clay Court Championships. I decided to suggest something radical to her before the All-American Championships. I challenged her to serve and volley behind all first serves, and to attack the net behind all second serve returns throughout the tournament. Kelly had not been a serve-and-volleyer. Her volley was decent, but she'd never spent much time at the net.

This was a way to fast-track her development as a more offensive player, but it was a lot to ask of a player who had already achieved a high level of success. In a team sport, athletes can make changes that simply alter their roles. Tennis players, like boxers, are on their own. By accepting this challenge, Kelly would be making herself extremely vulnerable. Many players would respond to this type of challenge by openly rebelling, or by complying begrudgingly only to resort to some type of passive-aggressive rebellion if things didn't work out in the short term.

Kelly chose to accept the challenge because that's what competitors do—thrive when challenged to move out of their comfort zones. Embracing discomfort is required to overachieve. I made sure to convey to Kelly that I believed she could overcome whatever limitations she perceived. She knew I believed in her ability to use her slice backhand as a weapon—one that could force opponents to give her opportunities to hit her forehand and take control of points. In the All-American, Kelly lost in the first round again, attacking the net relentlessly throughout. The next year, however, she returned and won the All-American Championships in decisive fashion, playing with newfound aggression. Her performance helped set the stage for a dramatic finish to a magical season that ended with our second national championship.

In college tennis, coaches are evaluated based on where their teams finish. The spring season when teams play dual matches is when the rubber hits the road. At the time, dual matches involved teams playing six singles matches and three doubles matches, with each match counting as one point. The first team to reach five points won.

As seniors, Kelly and Lucie provided tremendous leadership for a team that relied heavily on first- and second-year students. In the early rounds of the NCAA Championships, these young players performed well, defeating a tough Arizona State team in the Elite

Eight, and perennial powerhouse Stanford in the semifinals. But against number-one-ranked Florida, their youth and inexperience showed.

The finals of a tournament in any sport always feel starkly different from all of the previous rounds. It's like going into the final sales meeting to close the deal with a prospect you've been working on for months. It's as if the furniture in the meeting room has been rearranged. During the singles, our first-year players were like deer caught in the headlights. They lost their matches at number-four, number-five, and number-six singles, all three matches in straight sets within an hour, putting us down zero to three. Our sophomore, Farley Taylor, put the first point on the board with a clutch win at number-three singles. Lucie lost a brutally tough match to another tough competitor, Dawn Buth, at number-two singles. Lucie and Dawn had squared off like two boxers exchanging body blows over fifteen brutal rounds.

The score was now four to two. We were on the brink of defeat. Florida needed one more point.

Kelly was in a titanic battle at number-one singles with another elite competitor, Jill Craybas. She fell behind three to two in the third set and seemed to be fading. She was beginning to play conservatively, reverting to her old style of play. She needed a jolt, so I decided to have a few words with her on the changeover. I sat down next to her and was very direct.

"You have worked so hard over four years to develop the ability to dictate points. Hit your slice crosscourt, then knife it down the line. Make her dig it out of the ground, run around your backhand, move her with your forehand, and get to the net. Close this thing out!"

Once again, Kelly responded to the challenge by raising her level of competitiveness to win four straight games, closing out the match to make the team score four to three. The team was still alive!

The problem now was that we would have to sweep the doubles to beat Florida. No team had ever pulled that off in the history of NCAA Championship finals. Sweeping a great team in doubles was very difficult to do in a regular season match, let alone under the klieg lights of an NCAA Championship final.

But I felt good about our chances. During the regular season, we had encountered an unusually high number of rainy days, which was a problem because we didn't have indoor courts. Our only option on rainy days was to try to get to the one indoor, multipurpose tartan court in Bellmont Hall before the students who wanted to play badminton showed up. If we were fortunate enough to get there first, we then had to pull an old tennis net out of the closet and jury-rig it to two poles designed to hold volleyball nets. Tartan floors are very slick, which is not ideal for tennis, and this particular tartan floor was very old and worn. Trying to work on anything involving ground strokes was pointless because the ball would just skid erratically when it hit the surface. Thus, playing singles in Bellmont was not a viable option, but in my mind it was perfect for working on doubles. That's because in high-level doubles, you don't want to let the ball touch the ground; you want to make your opponents hit the ball off the ground, forcing them to pop it up as you close in to put the ball away with a volley or an overhead.

We worked hard on keeping the ball down and closing, as I repeated ad nauseam, "Find the ground and close!" We did an inordinate number of drills to work on this, including "crazy overheads," a drill I had created while at Colorado that involved feeding players fifteen to twenty lobs of all types at a quick clip, many at ridiculously extreme angles and trajectories. They had to hit every ball as an overhead, even balls that they would normally let bounce or hit as volleys. This drill not only improved the range and quality of their overheads, but it also instilled confidence in their ability to take anything out of the air and put it away. It gave them the feeling that they owned the net.

Kelly's clutch win had kept us alive, and by decisively winning four straight games to close it out, she pumped new life into her teammates. They rushed the court to congratulate her, but it wasn't time to celebrate yet. I knew that to win the match, I would need to bring them down to earth during the break, so they could reset and begin to focus on doubles. I directed them to a secluded area and left them alone so they could spread out, catch their breath, hydrate, and refocus. I let ten minutes pass, then walked over and pulled them together.

"Eyes here everybody! You have them right where you want them. It's time to go out and execute the way you have prepared to execute. Remember Bellmont!"

Kelly Pace and Cristina Moros won quickly at number-one doubles, as Kelly screamed encouragement to her teammates between points. Lucie Ludvigova and Ashley Johnson took a little longer, but also won at number-three doubles. Sophomore Farley Taylor, who had won a crucial singles match, was paired with first-year student Anne Pastor at number-two doubles. Farley and Anne were an up and down team, having produced a record that was barely above .500. They were our shakiest team. Every match had been an adventure during the regular season.

Now, they faced their ultimate adventure. Out of 286 Division I teams, Texas and Florida were the last two standing, and number-two doubles would decide which team went home a national champion.

Buoyed by the performance of the other two teams who flanked them on adjacent courts, Anne and Farley were on fire in the first set, winning decisively. Their surge surprised their Gator opponents, Craybas and Merchant, but the Florida duo gradually recovered, and Farley and Anne began to fade. Craybas and Merchant won the second set just as decisively as they had lost the first set. The first two sets seemed like two different matches altogether.

Because of their inconsistency as a team, and their lack of experience in NCAA tournaments, I coached Farley and Anne on virtually every point, calling serves, returns, and poaches as a catcher calls pitches. This was uncharacteristic for me. Unlike many coaches, I believed that matches were won in practice and found no added value in micromanaging my players during matches. What the team had worked on during those rainy days in Bellmont would carry over. For example, Kelly and Cristina were on a roll at number-one doubles. Any attempt to coach them could have derailed their momentum. Both assistant coaches were terrific. Vicki Ellis provided unrelenting support on all three courts. Kimm Ketelsen was on court with the number-three team, Lucie and Ashley, who did not mesh perfectly as a doubles team, but who were both seniors with experience in these situations. During her four years there, Ashley had been part of numerous doubles teams that had clinched hugely significant matches in NCAA Championship play. Lucie, on the other hand, was not a great doubles player. She was just plain tough!

The third set at number two was very tight throughout. As it progressed, Anne seemed to become progressively more nervous, which is not unusual for a young player in her first NCAA Championships. As if on cue, Farley started to take control. It was as if a switch had been flipped, and she started competing with the same wave of ferocity that had spurred her to a clutch victory in singles.

Farley had been another one of my under-the-radar recruits. She was from Montana, and had not played as many tournaments as most of her peers, but she was a superbly gifted athlete who had been a star Little League pitcher—that is, once the league had allowed her to participate. She moved swiftly and gracefully, earning the nickname "Bambi." Her backhand was anemic, but that often didn't matter because she was able to run around it to pounce with her explosive forehand. Her serve was also powerful. True to her roots as a baseball pitcher, she hit fastballs on the tennis court as well. In college, she responded to the much higher level of competition by learning to better locate her "fastballs," which kept her opponents off-balance.

As the third set progressed, Farley became increasingly aggressive, exploiting her Gator opponents' weaknesses with her serve, and running around backhands to hurt them with her forehand. At three to three, in the third set, Farley took *full* control. At fifteen to fifteen, she was about to serve to Craybas in the deuce court. Jill was vulnerable to wide serves to her forehand, but I sensed that she would lean that way, like a batter protecting the outside corner. I believed that it was time for a brush back pitch, so I instructed Farley to serve into body. She looked at me with a steely gaze and said, "Coach, I got this!" I turned to my assistant Kimm Ketelsen and said, "Wow. I think *we* got this!" Farley had taken charge!

Farley proceeded to hit an ace up the "T," as Jill leaned in the other direction. Two points later, Farley served to Jill again at forty to fifteen, and approached the net. Instead of hitting a crosscourt return, Jill attempted a lob over Anne, who was at the net as server's partner. Anne had hit more than enough crazy overheads in Bellmont to handle it, but she tightened up, let it go, and said, "Yours!" As Craybas and her partner rushed the net to close out the point, Farley made a mad dash for the baseline. She was negotiating a very awkward angle for a right-hander coming from the right side and moving diagonally backward while attempting to run around her backhand. But she was on fire and in full Bambi mode. She got there and pasted a forehand between the Gators at the net to hold serve, making the score four to three. Farley and Anne rode the resulting momentum to close out their match, completing a miraculous comeback.

Everyone rushed the court. I remember thinking how strange I felt because the first wave of thoughts that came into my head had nothing to do with the trophy we were about to receive. Instead, all I could think about was all the work the team had put into getting there.

Allan Burns, an Emmy Award–winning writer, was in attendance with his wife, Joan. They were longtime supporters and good friends. As Allan walked on the court to congratulate the team, he said, "There could be a movie made about this." Mike Warren, the point guard with teammate Lew Alcindor (Kareem Abdul-Jabbar) on four NCAA Championship teams, and a star on the hit TV series *Hill Street Blues,* was also at the match. He was so enthralled with the competitiveness of our team that he continued to follow Kelly's progress throughout the individual championships.

Kelly moved out of her comfort zone to achieve well beyond expectations. By accepting the challenge to overhaul her game, she truly embodied a spirit of Strivership. She had responded proactively to adversity that would have derailed the career of most athletes.

Kelly and Lucie provided leadership for a very young team by inspiring its members to imagine how good they could become. They were committed to striving together, and the results took care of themselves.

Champions versus Winners

Several years before our second title, a tradition of overachievement had been well established in the Texas program. This was due to a remarkable group of Strivers led by Carla Cossa, Susan Gilchrist, and Vickie Paynter, which resulted in the program's first NCAA Championship. The torch was then passed to Kelly Pace and Lucie Ludvigova, who fed off the momentum and led the program to a second NCAA title. People were drawn to these teams because of the way they competed. They exuded a kind of competitive charisma. These two teams, along with other overachieving teams that I was fortunate to be a part of, had one thing in common: they all had a strong core of athletes who led the way, fueled by a spirit of Strivership. They were driven by a shared commitment to stretch themselves to achieve beyond all expectations.

So, how can organizations in business, education, and sports build teams that consistently overachieve? Their leaders must make a fundamental decision: Do I want to build a winning organization or a championship organization? Do I want to build winning teams or championship teams? Do I want to achieve or overachieve?

Winning teams are built from the outside in. The focus is strictly on results. Decisions are made after asking questions such as: How will this make us look? How does it feel? And, most importantly: How will we compare with the Competition? Winning teams project an obsession with comparing favorably.

Championship teams, on the other hand, are driven by a purpose that transcends winning. They are built from the inside out. Decisions are made after asking, "Will this make us better?" A championship team is not always the team that wins the championship. I've coached teams that have won conference championships just because we had far superior talent. A true championship team is one that overachieves. Championship teams exude a Spirit of Strivership. These teams have a strong core of Strivers—team members who are wholly immersed in the process of getting better. When you are around Strivers, you can sense their excitement about getting better, every day, together.

There are two types of people in the world: Strivers and Arrivers. Strivers are typically the top performers in an organization because they are driven by a purpose that transcends winning. Strivers are driven to move themselves, their team, and their organization to achieve beyond all expectations. They have what to many people seems like a counterintuitive perspective on goal setting. For Strivers, achieving a goal is like passing a mile marker en route to a destination they never expect to reach. They use momentum from achieving a goal as motivation to go after their next challenge. Figuratively speaking, if I am a Striver and you challenge me to climb to the next plateau, I'm going to keep climbing until I'm at the top of the mountain. I may even fail to reach, much less surpass my goal. Strivers understand that they cannot control outcomes, but they are always focused on reaching beyond their grasp.

Solving new and complex problems is what makes Strivers tick. They are always moving from the actual to the possible. This inevitably creates tension, which breeds discomfort, but a state of discomfort is where people grow and where seemingly intractable problems are solved.

When I say the word *Striver*, most people assume I am talking about a corporate titan or world leader, like Steve Jobs or Nelson Mandela. But Strivers exist in every walk of life. The housekeepers at Four Seasons Hotels are Strivers. Their performance is evaluated based on their ability to make the customer experience special. Unlike at other hotels, Four Seasons housekeepers are not just hired to clean rooms. They are hired following multiple interviews structured to determine whether they are willing to strive together to ensure that each customer's experience is special.

So, what does a housekeeper at the Four Seasons have in common with someone like the late Steve Jobs, who some might say was an over-the-top Striver? They are both driven by a purpose that transcends winning. They are always reaching beyond their grasp.

Arrivers, on the other hand, are the opposite of Strivers. They hesitate to reach beyond their grasp and start to panic as soon as success is not within clutching distance. Arrivers pour most of their energy into creating a perception of greatness rather than actually persevering to achieve greatness. In business terms, they prioritize branding over product development. Arrivers will develop their product, but only to the degree that it embellishes the impression they want to create.

Arrivers do not compete. They aren't concerned with bettering themselves, only with how their results will compare to others. This is all too common these days. The term *results-oriented* has morphed into *results-obsessed*. Any result will do—whatever it takes to compare favorably to the competition. Arrivers are not fueled by continuous improvement; they're driven by the pursuit of promotions, grades, trophies, awards, or anything that will enable them to compare favorably to others.

Most business leaders are aware of the groundbreaking work done by Laszlo Bock, Google's first chief people officer. His approach to human resources at Google completely changed the HR landscape. Bock decided to analyze the background of Google's top performers. He assumed that the vast majority of their top performers received excellent grades in college. However, research found little correlation between the grades employees received and their performance at Google. Consequently, Google no longer looks at transcripts. In fact, on some teams at Google, 14 percent of employees did not even graduate from college.[4]

Think about what this changing landscape means. Arrivers feel they will succeed in life simply because they have a degree from a prestigious school. They hang their hats on their degrees and academic honors, which sets them up for disaster in an age when success is determined not by what you know, but by what you do with your knowledge.

Leaders in every walk of life quote the late John Wooden, legendary UCLA basketball coach, whom many consider the best coach in the history of sports. He once said, "Be more concerned with your character than your reputation, because your character is what you really are, while your reputation is merely what others think you are."

To borrow from Wooden, Arrivers are driven by who people think they are. They want to control their reputation by any means possible. Arrivers are masters of impression management, an industry that has exploded in recent years. Their focus is on *personal branding*, a term that didn't even exist a generation ago. We used to brand commodities, like cereal and soap; now we brand people. We're living in a world that has succumbed to an Arriver Mentality, a world obsessed with style over substance.

People used to say your reputation is all that you have. Arrivers have distorted this by viewing reputation as all-important. They work from the outside in. Strivers see reputation as an extension of their character; a Striver's reputation flows from the inside out.

---

4   Adam Bryant, "In Head-Hunting, Big Data May Not Be Such A Big Deal: An Interview with Laszlo Bock," *New York Times*, June 19, 2013, https://www. nytimes.com/2013/06/20/business/in-head-hunting-big-data-may-not-be-such-a-big-deal.html?module=inline.

I'm often asked if people are destined to be either Strivers or Arrivers. Is a person inevitably going to become one or the other? The truth is, for each of us, it is a bit of a roller coaster. No one feels like striving all the time. A myriad of factors and reasons can affect us, like experiencing a personal tragedy, or dealing with disappointment after a major failure. As a result, in either case, we might lose our drive to compete.

Even renowned titans like Steve Jobs rode that roller coaster. We remember him as the tech mogul who changed the world, but at one point, Steve Jobs was effectively kicked out of Apple—the company he had co-founded. He became a defeatist. He spoke about giving up and leaving the country. For a time, he became an Arriver. He was human like everyone else, and life had knocked him down. Life can cause all of us to sink into the Valley of Arrivers from time to time.

My Personal Roller Coaster

I, too, have ridden the roller coaster of striving and arriving during my career. Before coming to Texas, I coached at the University of Colorado. At that time, CU was not exactly at the epicenter of college tennis. We had very few of the advantages that other Division I programs enjoyed. We had only three and a half scholarships, whereas virtually every other program had the maximum of eight. My salary was very small and I had to work a part-time job on the side, teaching and coaching in Denver.

In addition to not having the same advantages, we had some unique disadvantages, the biggest of which being our altitude. Boulder is at a high altitude, a contrast with most of our opponents, who were at sea level. The air is thicker at sea level and thins out the higher you go. When you train in high altitude and then go to sea level, initially the air makes it feel as though you're swinging your racket through water. Everything feels sluggish, which makes competing at a high level very challenging.

We had to practice indoors from November through March. During my early years there, our practice time was at 6:00 a.m. We had to practice at a club with private members, and that was the only time we could reserve the courts. My days were exhausting: practice at 6:00 a.m., driving back and forth between Denver and Boulder for work, late nights preparing for the next practice, and making recruiting calls.

The coach before me had not been able to devote as much time or energy to the team because of her day job as a professor at CU. To me it wasn't a job. I was extremely passionate about my craft, tackling challenges with optimism, and always reaching beyond my grasp.

This youthful enthusiasm helped me cobble together recruiting classes, a combination of talented, under-the-radar first-year students and transfers. Colorado had begun to produce some excellent junior players, some of whom would initially go to schools with more prominent tennis programs on the West Coast. Many of them returned, homesick and looking forward to joining an up-and-coming program in their home state.

The only "blue chip" recruit I signed at CU was Allison Macatee, a top-twenty player from Northern Virginia. Allison was a talented player, but she also possessed unusual qualities for a tennis athlete. Tennis is brutally difficult to master, and you're on your own—no subs! This pressure often produces self-absorbed players who have never been part of a team. Allison, however, was very comfortable in her own skin, and also related well with her teammates.

Unfortunately, Allison was only with us for a short time. Her roommate, a member of the track team, lived in a nearby town. One night she invited Allison to her home for dinner. On the way they approached a hill. Driving up the other side of the hill was an elderly man. As he approached the top of the hill, he suffered a heart attack and lost control of his car. Allison's roommate was driving and reflexively turned the vehicle sharply to the left. Allison, who was in the passenger seat, was struck and died instantly.

We were all devastated by the loss of an extraordinary person whom we'd barely gotten to know.

The United States Tennis Association decided to create a new sportsmanship award in her honor, to be awarded at the USTA Indoor National Junior Championships in Plainville, Massachusetts, the following fall. I was asked to attend and present the award. When I arrived, I was warmly welcomed by tournament officials, but many of the players and their parents were taken aback. They did not know why I was there and assumed I was recruiting. At that time, college coaches did not go to tournaments to recruit. The only other coach in attendance was Alice Tym from nearby Yale. Parents were wary of us, as if we were traveling salespeople prepared to distract their daughters with our recruiting sales pitches.

I *was* also there to recruit Allison's doubles partner, Kathleen Cummings. Prior to her accident, Allison had been aggressively reaching out to Kathleen, hoping that they could play together at Colorado. So, I had already been in contact with Kathleen. As it turns out, the recipient of the Allison Macatee Sportsmanship Award was determined by a vote of the players participating in the tournament, and Kathleen Cummings got the most votes.

Kathleen was not a blue-chip recruit. Her national ranking, which was in the forties during most of her junior career, would not attract the attention of today's Division I coaches. The pool of talented young American players is very shallow today. But the country was in the middle of a tennis boom during Kathleen's junior career. Many of her peers—players like Andrea Jaeger, Tracy Austin, and Pam Shriver—would soon become top pros. Kathleen selected Colorado, arrived on campus the following fall, and in a remarkably short time came out of nowhere to join Jaeger, Austin, and Shriver in the history books. In her first two years at Colorado, she improved from a top forty junior player to a ranking of forty-eighth in the world among *all* female players. She accomplished this by transforming her game with prodigious focus and determination.

Kathleen was the epitome of a Striver. She was not blessed with a lot of natural ability. She was not a great mover, and all but one of her strokes was distinctly average. The exception was her backhand, which many thought was the best two-hand backhand in the world at the time. Unlike her serve and forehand, which appeared stiff and awkward, she attacked her backhand with a long, ferocious swing. Then she learned to use her other strokes tactically to get backhands. When she got one, her eyes would bug out as if to say to her opponent, "I'm going to punish you for hitting it there. Get ready to run!" I have never seen an athlete get more out of her ability than Kathleen Cummings. She exhibited a spirit of Strivership every day in practice, hitting what seemed like every shot with purpose.

After we snuck into the top twenty-five, I decided to start hosting an indoor tournament with seven of the top teams in the country, with the goal of promoting our program. Most of the tournament was held at the same indoor club where we practiced. I approached people at Coors about sponsoring the event. My timing was good because the brewer had just launched a new product, *Coors Light*, a couple of years earlier. The company agreed to sponsor the tournament *and* to serve Coors Light. As you might well imagine, this attracted plenty of college students, who created a tremendous home court advantage.

In the first round of the tournament we upset Trinity University, the number-two team in the country. The atmosphere was so electric that Denver TV stations interrupted their nightly news broadcasts to deliver updates on Kathleen Cummings's match at number-one singles. If we had played Trinity outdoors at sea level, the competition would have destroyed us in short order. But indoors, at night, at six thousand feet, with a standing-room-only crowd going nuts, we were able to pull out a great team victory.

We played the finals of the tournament at the Old Balch Field-house, which at the time had a tartan floor. I arranged to rent a court from a company in Atlanta that was used for professional tournaments. The court arrived by truck on campus with little time to spare. After we had rolled it out, we discovered that there were wrinkles everywhere, including on the seams that connected the pieces of the court. What had I been thinking? I had rented a court sight unseen, assuming that it would look just like the courts rolled out for the pro tournaments I'd watched on TV. This was going to be easy, right? But my twentysomething hubris had gotten me in trouble.

This particular court had been rolled up in storage for months. The court was unplayable, and the finals of the tournament were only a week away. Fortunately, I was able to find a veteran jack-of-all-trades handyman in Denver who had experience in situations like this. He traveled to Boulder and worked long hours using special tools to transform the court into acceptable shape. During the finals, I remember crossing my fingers and praying that the ball would not land on certain seams that would have yielded a crazy bounce. Somehow we got through the event.

I was obsessed with building a competitive program at CU, and it worked. Within three years, things were really turning around. That's when the administration offered me the coaching position on the men's team as well. For me, it was a great opportunity: I would get to do more of what I loved, I would get paid a decent salary, and I would no longer need part-time jobs. Of course, my life only got crazier. Despite the fact that I was now coaching two teams, I only had one part-time assistant. I didn't let any of it bother me, though; when you're in your twenties you don't know what you don't know yet, and everything seems possible.

For the first part of my career in Colorado, I was striving. The roller coaster had me riding high. However, as roller coasters do, it was about to throw me for a loop.

Our success at CU opened up other opportunities for me. The last year that I hosted our indoor tournament, I went to the airport to pick up the North Carolina team. On the way back, the opposing coach, Kitty Harrison, said to me, "Did you know the Texas job is open?" She happened to be a Texas alum and thought I should go for the job. I didn't think I had a chance and told her as much, but as soon as I dropped her team off at their hotel, I called my administrative assistant, and asked her to throw together my resume and FedEx it to Texas.

I landed an interview, but I had thrown my hat into the ring very late and was up against some stiff competition. I was up against coaches who were older, and who had teams in the top ten. My team was ranked twentieth. We had exceeded all expectations, but I was definitely the underdog candidate.

I interviewed well and was offered the job.

Now I am at *the* University of Texas. This is the big time—I'm twenty-nine years old and I'm in the Promised Land. All of a sudden,

I am at a school that has great facilities, terrific weather, and a tremendous athletics tradition. At the time, most of the other coaches in the department had been or were about to become an Olympic coach in their sport and almost all of them had won national championships. Surely, I could succeed in this amazing environment after overachieving in less-than-ideal conditions at Colorado.

Our program, however, had not been keeping up. I was the fourth tennis coach the school had hired in seven years. It was very intimidating to be new in that environment and feel the pressure to catch up to these more experienced, highly accomplished coaches.

So, I did what seemed to make the most sense, at least to those outside the college coaching realm. I decided I was going to attract the best possible talent by selling the University of Texas. I was going to go into a recruit's home and say, "You're special. You deserve to be at a place like Texas. Look at all that we have to offer you. We're going to win a national championship and you're going to be a big part of it." I enticed them to come to Texas by promoting the Texas brand. That was the perfect business plan. As far as administrators, the media, and the fans are concerned, it still is considered the perfect business plan. I was a young, naïve upstart from Colorado. How could I argue with them?

Unfortunately, the "perfect" business plan failed miserably. In my first six years at Texas, we underachieved by Texas standards. In my early years, all of the women's programs at Texas were expected to be in the top ten, and we were languishing in the bottom of the top twenty. I was struggling and feeling that I was in way over my head.

Then came the low point. Our athletics director at the time was Dr. Donna Lopiano—a remarkable woman who had been a key advocate in the fight to pass Title IX legislation. Donna was fiercely competitive and held everyone, from entry-level workers to administrators, to a high standard. It seemed like everyone I dealt with in the department was at the top of his or her field.

Donna had given a speech to a business group downtown, and one of our program's supporters had been in attendance. He reported to me that during the Q and A, someone asked her, "You say you want all of your teams in the top ten. What about tennis?" Donna apparently responded by saying she was "going to take care of that."

On one hand, I was not happy to hear this because it had not been directly expressed to me. On the other hand, how could I argue?

At Texas, my teams were expected to contend for national championships. But despite all the advantages I had, the Longhorn program was in worse shape than it had been when I arrived. I was miserable and the stress continued to build until I was on the verge of a nervous breakdown.

Fortunately, I got a wake-up call. During the first team meeting at the beginning of my seventh year we were talking about what we were going to work on that year, when one of the athletes suddenly raised her hand.

"Our practices are not motivating. There's not enough variety," she said.

Now, that was not necessarily an unusual comment, but at that point in time, it struck a chord. I remember firing back, "Winning colors everything, and right now, we're not winning. We're not winning by Texas standards because we're not practicing winning."

It felt so good, like something had been lifted off my shoulders. But that night, I realized what word I had said four times: *winning*. Suddenly, I realized I had been listening to too many other people in the department tell me how to run my program. I was concerned with my reputation and had become obsessed with results. I was working from the outside in, rather than from the inside out.

I had become an Arriver. I had put together a beautiful package with a beautiful bow on it, but there was nothing inside. Now I was angry at myself, but also pumped. At Colorado, I had prepared athletes to become competitors. At Texas, I had been preparing athletes to play.

I realized that since competition is uncomfortable, my practices needed to become uncomfortable. I define competition in sports as making the opposition uncomfortable with purpose-driven execution.

Competing is not about working hard; hard work is strictly task-oriented and linear. It's about grinding. It's what is expected of athletes in the weight room or the classroom. Competition does require energy, but it is not all about energy. In sports today, there is often way too much aimless energy during practice, and even during competitions. Go to any college or high school sport practice today, and you will be struck by the cacophony of false positives. "Good job!" they shout, even if a teammate is simply *doing her job*. Every single execution elicits a remark. This creates a catch-22: if you don't say "good shot" after every good shot, players will look around as if they are expecting praise. If you do say "good shot" every time, then it starts to lack meaning.

So, I began designing practices to become more competitive by creating scenarios that challenged our athletes to solve problems. I created an Uncomfort Zone.

It worked. Two years post-epiphany, the team became the lowest-seeded team to ever advance to the Final Four. Two years later,

> *I began designing practices to become more competitive by creating scenarios that challenged our athletes to solve problems.*

the team upset Stanford to advance to the NCAA finals, breaking Stanford's fifty-three-match home win streak and its string of five consecutive national titles. It was heralded as one of the biggest upsets in college sports that year. But the team was devastated when we lost a very close match to Florida in the finals. The team wanted to win it all.

The following year, the team became the lowest-seeded team to win an NCAA Championship in college tennis. Our program went on to appear in three more Elite Eights, make two more Final Fours, advance to the finals again, and capture another national championship. More importantly, the team overachieved in all but one of those accomplishments by finishing ahead of where it was seeded.

Why did these teams overachieve? They were committed to competing—to striving together—in practice every day to make each other better. I was very fortunate to have the opportunity to be around athletes who arrived at practice every day with "I want to get better today" written all over their faces. These athletes generated a Spirit of Strivership every day in practice.

Championship teams do not focus externally on the Competition. They embrace a spirit of Strivership. By focusing on competing internally, they are ready for anything the Competition throws at them.

CHAPTER FOUR

WHY STRIVERSHIP MATTERS

Major employers are all looking for the same thing—people who can invent, adapt, and reinvent their jobs every day.

—Thomas Friedman

Strivership is in our nation's DNA. Our founding fathers embraced the underlying principles of Strivership in the construction of our federal government. As renowned historian James Ellis noted, "The Constitution was intended less to resolve arguments than to make argument itself the solution." That doesn't fit your typical let's-all-get-along collaborative model. The founders wanted ideas to *compete*, and they knew that allowing for that to happen would ultimately strengthen our nation. This competition of ideas was in pursuit of our common betterment. American democracy would be defined not by simply working together, but by striving together to achieve beyond expectations. That's what has made the US exceptional.

> "The Constitution was intended less to resolve arguments than to make argument itself the solution."

Ellis wrote that to facilitate such competition of ideas, ambiguities were purposefully embedded into our constitution. Ambiguity, as I have previously pointed out, is where Strivers thrive. In the post–Industrial Age, ambiguity is increasingly a part of our everyday lives. Change has accelerated, and that means we can no longer rely on variables at hand to solve problems. Problem solving is no longer a straightforward process. The time when you could simply apply some elbow grease to solve most problems now seems like a quaint notion.

In today's world of ambiguity, we don't know what is coming next. The only constant is *exponential* change. Innovation is accelerating at a pace that would have seemed unimaginable during the Industrial Age. Product cycles once lasted decades; now they are measured in years, even months. The automobile was invented in 1886, yet the interstate highway system wasn't built until the 1950s. Compare that to Facebook, which didn't exist prior to 2004. Fifteen years later, not only is this "highway system" built, but more than two billion people are using it. In today's volatile marketplace, as soon as you finish designing a revolutionary new technology, you must begin upgrading it, or working on something new. Just look at the iPhone, and Apple's never-ending race to stay ahead of the technology curve. The company is always working on the next generation of its flagship product.

In previous generations, if you had a college degree you could find a very good job, and possibly work for the same company your entire career. In that world, you could be an Arriver and get by nicely. If you were willing to work hard to compare favorably, you could stop working at sixty-five and retire with a healthy pension.

Young people today are entering a workplace that is much more disruptive and unpredictable. Working hard has become a minimal requirement, and Arrivers get left behind. Change is occurring at a rate we could not have imagined a generation ago. Some projections indicate that today's young people will have up to twenty-five jobs during their careers.[5] The standard full-time-with-benefits jobs are quickly disappearing as we move toward a part-time, project-based economy. Studies suggest that 85 percent of the jobs available in 2030 haven't even been invented yet. And by 2027, many expect over 50 percent of the workforce will be freelancers.[6] *Freelancing* used to be a term primarily associated with writers or graphic designers. Now the corporate world is outsourcing jobs of all types. Technological innovation is reshaping the way we interact with one another and the way we do business.

The Constitution was not designed to offer clear answers. You could say the same thing today about our economy. There are no clear answers, and to succeed in this environment, you must compete. When young people leave the cocoon and enter this disruptive, unstable environment, it can be a tremendous shock to their system. In school, they've been conditioned to be Arrivers. They know how

---

5   Jeanne Meister, "The Future Of Work: Job Hopping Is the 'New Normal' for Millennials," *Forbes*, August 14, 2012, https://www.forbes.com/sites/jeannemeister/2012/08/14/the-future-of-work-job-hopping-is-the-new-normal-for-millennials/#6ac6769a13b8.

6   Elaine Pofeldt, "Are We Ready for a Workforce that Is 50% Freelance?" *Forbes*, October 17, 2017, https://www.forbes.com/sites/elainepofeldt/2017/10/17/are-we-ready-for-a-workforce-that-is-50-freelance/#2ec8baf23f82.

to play the game of school, grinding for grades by using established methods to find solutions that teachers are expecting. Then suddenly, they're thrust into a twenty-first-century economy, where they are challenged to solve problems unconventionally because many of the problems they're confronted with do not have established solutions. It's like a notification pops up on an ever-present screen with an urgent question: Are you going to compare or compete?

A sense of urgency to rediscover our ethic of Strivership was reinforced for me when I read *A Whole New Mind,* by Daniel Pink. The new world needs creative problem solvers who are lifelong learners. Pink supports this notion by arguing that the future belongs to a new kind of thinker. Whereas logical, "left-brain" thinkers were successful in the past, the future will be defined by creative, "right-brain" thinkers.[7]

The left brain is detail oriented. It handles logic, sequence, and analysis, meaning it is good at breaking things down into parts. When change was more incremental and product cycles were longer, left-brain abilities sufficed. They allowed you to master the processes required to chart a linear path to success in the workplace.

Now that technology and innovation are disrupting businesses and entire industries, right-brain thinking gives you an edge because the right brain is wired for understanding context, making you adept at knowing how things fit together. You are able to connect isolated elements to create a big-picture view of the landscape.

Right-brain thinkers are in tune with emotional expression, which fuels creativity. Conventional logic holds that left-brain thinkers are better at succeeding in business, sports, and school because they are

---

7   Daniel Pink, *A Whole New Mind: Why Right-Brainers Will Rule the Future* (New York: Riverhead Books, 2006).

capable of analyzing, being methodical, and mastering processes. In today's business world, MFAs are the new MBAs.

There's no how-to book on creative problem solving. You can't codify it or break it down into simple steps. You can't study other leaders and copy what they did, because every disruption and every obstacle is unique. Pink refers to this new era as the "Conceptual Age." The world needs workers who use both sides of the brain. But, whereas left-brain thinkers may have dominated the Information Age, the Conceptual Age is about adaptation, understanding, and empathy. In a world of constant change, we need people who thrive when challenged to solve novel problems.

Pink explains that for most of human history, scarcity has defined our lives. But now abundance is a defining feature of social, economic, and cultural interaction. This abundance has done two things: it's made left-brain thinking less valued, and it has created generations that are searching for purpose.

In this new age of abundance, rational appeals and logical processes are not enough. Yes, engineers still need to be skilled at analysis and finding ways to make things work. However, functionality is no longer enough. Now, things need functionality and emotional appeal. It has to be visually pleasing and possibly even connect to a larger message.

In a stable and predictable world, competing—striving together—was considered key to staying ahead of the game. The question was whether you were willing to work hard enough, and the goal was simply to compare favorably.

In a world of rapid change, organizations in all industries must embrace an ethos of Strivership. Now, striving together is required to stay in the game. People must be prepared to invent, adapt, and reinvent their jobs every day.

Business Is a Team Sport

Remember, an embrace of Strivership means that you are competing in more than Relationship to Self. At Texas and Colorado, I knew we could become championship teams in a given year if everyone involved, from athletes to coaches, was striving together in Relationships to Self, Team, and Boss. And since I was the boss, the pressure was on for me to strive together in Relationship to Direct Reports (athletes). The same is true in today's corporate world. More than ever before, businesses are working in teams. This includes freelancer gigs, where working on a team and reporting to a boss are often the reality. Freelancers just change teams more often.

In Relationship to Self, you're striving together—competing with yourself—if you thrive when challenged to move out of your comfort zone to problem-solve unconventionally, and you learn new things while persevering through the inevitable setbacks that you encounter in the process.

In Relationship to Team, you're striving together if you thrive when challenged to be assertive with teammates during team meetings. Strivers also support their teammates unconditionally to all outside entities without exception. Internally, they offer complete support as well, unless a serious problem arises—in which case, they communicate directly with the source in a timely manner.

In Relationship to Boss, you're striving together if you thrive when challenged to offer the boss new ideas. Strivers also support the boss unconditionally to all outside entities without exception. Internally, they offer complete support as well, unless a serious problem arises—in which case, they communicate directly with the boss in a timely manner.

When Laszlo Bock was at Google, the company was looking for competitors—people who were willing to strive together. He said,

"What we've seen is that the people who are the most successful here, who we want to hire, will have a fierce position. They'll argue like hell. They'll be zealots about their point of view."[8]

You need a strong ego drive, humility, and empathy in the same person.

I wanted to help other leaders understand the value of the qualities that Bock was looking for, and show them how to uncover those characteristics themselves. That's why I developed the Striver Quotient® Assessment Tool to help leaders identify Striver Attributes in both their existing workforce and among their prospective job candidates. I wanted to give companies and teams a tool for assessing Strivership that broke it down into tangible, actionable attributes.

> *"What we've seen is that the people who are the most successful here, who we want to hire, will have a fierce position. They'll argue like hell. They'll be zealots about their point of view."*

The Striver Quotient®

In the corporate world, surveys continue to report that 46 percent of all new hires fail within eighteen months.[9] That's staggering to think about. How can this be happening with all of the innovation dedicated to identifying successful hires? Imagine how much capital

---

8   Thomas L. Friedman, "How to Get a Job at Google," *New York Times*, February 22, 2004, https://www.nytimes.com/2014/02/23/opinion/sunday/friedman-how-to-get-a-job-at-google.html.

9   Leadership IQ, "Why New Hires Fail (Emotional Intelligence vs. Skills)," June 22, 2015, https://www.leadershipiq.com/blogs/leadershipiq/35354241-why-new-hires-fail-emotional-intelligence-vs-skills.

is being expended to constantly train new hires, to say nothing about lost productivity. Why is this happening?

The problem is that too many companies are looking for A-players. If you're like most people, you're probably saying, "Wait a minute. Are you trying to tell me companies should hire B-players?" That sounds ridiculous, of course. But what makes someone an A-player, and are those attributes truly exceptional?

Think about what typically constitutes an A-player:

- high IQ

- excellent people skills (EQ)

- superior job skills

- strong work ethic

A person with those qualities is going to get the job done, no question about it. Some would go as far as to say A-players are the complete package. But are they Strivers? Are they wired to strive together or simply work together?

The problem is that Strivers do not view themselves as the complete package; they view themselves as incomplete. Strivers are constantly looking for ways to improve. They roll their eyes when they hear corporate buzzwords like *A-player*.

> *Strivers do not view themselves as the complete package; they view themselves as incomplete. Strivers are constantly looking for ways to improve.*

Most A-players know exactly what they have to do to earn that status. They check off the boxes necessary to achieve the A-player standard so they can compare favorably to others. They are not driven to achieve what appears to be beyond their grasp. They are merely seeking a seal of approval. The *A* stands for Arriver.

In an economy driven by constant innovation, the top performers on your team will be those who see themselves as incomplete, driven by a desire for continual improvement. A-players are not motivated to stretch because they have been ordained as a complete package.

Companies shouldn't be looking for A-players; they should be looking for Strivers. Take a look at the A-player attributes again. Not long ago, your IQ alone was considered to be the key to your success. Many companies actually tested for IQ in the hiring process, and some still do to this day. But an IQ score does not directly correlate to success in the twenty-first-century workplace. Intelligence is malleable.

Today, the same can be said about a person's people skills, or EQ. In the 1990s, Daniel Goleman pioneered the discussion about emotional intelligence. The idea was that businesses could improve their hiring processes and build better teams if they gauged and assessed not just intellectual capability, but also emotional intelligence. Thus, EQ was born. Businesses no longer had to depend on the one-dimensional factor that IQ represented. EQ criteria provided a much-needed upgrade to hiring processes. The notion of people skills became a game changer.

But in an age of innovation, people skills are no longer the key difference maker. We are seeing a rate of change that used to take decades to occur. We no longer live in a world of uncertainty with established variables always at hand to select from. In the past, a person with a high IQ could be called on to figure out which variable worked best. Another person who possessed strong EQ qualities could be called on to mobilize the team to execute.

Today, success in the workplace increasingly depends on one's ability to thrive in ambiguity. Imagine that I am the CEO of a tech company and you are my chief designer. You led the team that invented our flagship product, a technological advancement on par with the iPhone. I pull you into my office one day, less than six months after the product you designed went to market, and inform you that a developer on the other side of the globe has come up with a better prototype of your product.

Your work on this project reflects your brilliance, and your people skills, but it is once again time to get back to the drawing board. This product must be retooled.

A lot of people would be angry, even insulted. Who is this developer? In today's world, it doesn't matter how you compare on paper.

What's needed to succeed in such a scenario? IQ and EQ help us get to this point, but now we need something more.

Certainly, if we're designing smartphones or building rockets, we need people with higher-than-average IQs. But being the smartest person in a room full of smart people is not going to change the game. And, although people skills will always be important, the scenarios that leaders encounter with both direct reports and customers change more frequently and abruptly. Workplace environments used to be fairly predictable. A scripted persona, genuine or otherwise, sufficed. But Tom Friedman has reported that major employers are now looking for the same thing: "People who will invent, adapt, and reinvent their jobs every day."[10]

---

10   Thomas Friedman, "The Start-Up of You," *New York Times*, July 12, 2011, https://www.nytimes.com/2011/07/13/opinion/13friedman.html?mtrref=www.google.com.

To succeed in today's economy, workers must constantly adapt to a rapidly changing environment. A sense of urgency to rise to the occasion—to push themselves outside of their comfort zone and strive together—has become the key to success. It's now about how you respond to the constant challenge to go "back to the drawing board." I have developed a way to gauge those attributes. It's not your IQ or EQ, but your SQ—your *Striver Quotient*®—that is now the key differentiator.

Championship organizations in every industry embrace a spirit of Strivership. Their leaders seek to cultivate a willingness to strive together in their people. The first step in the process is to evaluate their Striver Quotient®.

CHAPTER FIVE

THE STRIVER QUOTIENT® ASSESSMENT

Human beings are complicated, thorny, messy things. But those unquantifiable qualities are also what make magic happen.

—Laszlo Bock

When millennials first began to appear on the recruiting trail in the late '90s, it became more challenging to identify Strivers. I found it much more difficult to find young people who expected more of themselves than I expected of them. I was operating from the inside out, but most recruits seemed to be operating from the outside in. Most had been conditioned to create a positive impression by building the best possible personal brand. Young people's lives were being stage-managed by their parents, who were always around and constantly intervening. This prevented me from building a strong relationship with each recruit.

I began using behavioral interviewing techniques with recruits in an effort to uncover any sign of a competitive edge that may be lying dormant beneath the surface. Behavioral interviewing involves asking questions about past behavior to predict future behavior. I started asking questions like:

- Describe a time when you were challenged to move out of your comfort zone by a practice partner. How did you respond?

- Tell me about a time when an opponent pushed you out of your comfort zone. How did you respond?

- Have you ever had to learn an entirely new skill? What was involved? How long did it take you to become reasonably proficient?

These types of questions were designed to build up to asking how they won points, which was a tough question for most tennis recruits to answer. They would typically respond by simply describing their game style. Realizing they had probably never considered this question, I would follow up by asking them how they got to the net when they played points. Oftentimes, their response would be, "I rarely make it to the net," which meant they still didn't understand what I was after. I would then ask them, "How do you try get to the net?" Most recruits remained perplexed. So, I got more specific by asking, "I know you rarely make it to the net, but do you construct points with the goal of getting there?"

The answer I was looking for was how they competed. What tactics did they employ to make their opponents uncomfortable with purpose-driven execution? For example, I might ask what their weapon is, and how they set up the point so they can use it. As is the case with most college sports today, coaches are dealing with recruits who know how to play, but not how to compete. Most tennis recruits arrive on campus having focused on how to hit shots, not how to use their shots to win points.

I would also ask recruits about past coaches, an important area of inquiry. Their responses often provided a window into the role that parents were playing in the recruiting process. At this point, parents would frequently interrupt to tell anecdotes about the coach who ruined their nine-year-old's forehand, or the coach who was not positive enough. As a younger coach, I would think, "Well, I'm not like that. They're going to love me!" And they did, until the results were not to their liking. As a more experienced coach, having now been burned enough times, I knew a relationship like this would not work. Eventually, I would be next on the chopping block!

I wanted each recruit to "select for" or "select out." I put recruits in a position that compelled them to make the decision. To close the deal, I would often use an approach that started by asking them to tell me about their toughest match in junior tennis. They would usually describe a long, tough, upset win in a big tournament over a player seeded much higher. I would respond by saying, "I was there, and your performance in that match is one reason I'm high on you, but I have an important question. If you come to Texas next August, are you prepared to compete like that every day in practice?"

A recruit's body language usually told me everything I needed to know. Some recruits would show signs of panic, as if their steady IV drip of affirmation was cut off.

I knew these recruits could *play*, but I needed to know if they would *compete*; there's a difference. I wanted to know, or at least sense, that recruits believed they were already accomplished, but had a burning desire to get better.

Though I did not realize it at the time, the behavioral interview questions I had devised for recruits became the foundation of the Striver Quotient® Assessment Tool that I use in my business today. I had developed the concepts that would form the basis of the Striver Quotient® Assessment while at Trinity Episcopal. There, we sought to cultivate a willingness to build strong Relationships to Self, Team, and Coach in young athletes.

After I left Trinity Episcopal to start my consulting business, I retained the services of Scott Liening in UT's psychology department to build the assessment tool. I wanted the assessment to be professionally constructed and statistically reliable. Scott helped me tweak the relationships and attributes, then went to work designing questions. The process of building a reliable assessment used to take several years, but with modern technology, Scott was able to get it done in under two years.

The Striver Quotient® Assessment Tool evaluates one's willingness to compete, to strive together, in three key relationships: Self, Team, and Boss/Coach. And people in an organization who have direct reports are assessed in a fourth relationship, Relationship to Direct Reports.

Scott had never seen an assessment like this, so he was highly invested in the development process. He explained that most instruments are personality assessments, which evaluate abstract qualities by measuring discrete personality traits. He told me that personality assessments can be beneficial by creating an awareness that leads to a deeper understanding of who you are. However, he said, "The limitation is that you cannot change who you are. You can only adapt your personality."

According to Scott, SQ is not a personality assessment because it measures performance attributes, which evaluate where you are, not who you are. Unlike personality assessments, SQ assessment results are tangible and actionable because you have the ability to change where you are—and your personality adapts in the process.

Because it is actionable, the Striver Quotient® Assessment is a catalyst for the work I do helping leaders build championship teams. When working with a team in business, sports, or education, I begin the process by asking each team member to take the SQ online. Their results are submitted internally, directly to my system. I want them to hear my presentation on Strivership before reviewing their profiles. I wrap up each presentation by providing a quick overview of what the assessment reveals by sketching this matrix on a whiteboard:

0	Cooperative (working alone)	Collaborative (working together)	Competitive (striving together)	100
Self	Certainty	Uncertainty	Ambiguity	
Team	Solo	Harmony	Tension	
Boss	Flexible	"Reachable goal" setter	"Stretch goal" setter	
D. Reports	N/A	"Reward me"	"Push me"	

As I sketch the matrix on the board, I talk about each term to explain what the Striver Quotient® Assessment is designed to measure. The matrix provides people with a framework that triggers questions about the concepts underlying what the SQ evaluates. The matrix also reveals one key attribute in each of the four relationships:

- In Relationship to Self: Strivers thrive when challenged to move out of their comfort zones.

- In Relationship to Team: Strivers are assertive and will challenge teammates.

- In Relationship to Boss: Strivers want a Boss who pushes them.

- In Relationship to Direct Reports: Strivers search for direct reports who want to be pushed.

After the discussion generated by the matrix, I sometimes divide team members into small groups and conduct breakout sessions to determine what they think are the essential attributes in each relationship before I pass out their SQ profiles. Other times, I will immediately pass out hard copies of everyone's SQ profile and begin the group review. Their profiles reveal where they are with respect to each Striver attribute.

In Relationship to Self, the willingness to:
- move outside your comfort zone

- solve difficult problems unconventionally

- learn new skills

- persevere through adversity

- present an accurate self-image

In Relationship to Team, the willingness to:
- be assertive and challenge teammates

- support teammates

- demonstrate empathy for teammates

- communicate directly in a timely manner with the source when issues arise with a teammate

In Relationship to Boss, the willingness to:
- be assertive by offering the boss new ideas

- support the boss

- communicate directly in a timely manner with the boss when an issue arises

In Relationship to Direct Reports, the willingness to:
- lead change

- encourage direct reports to stretch beyond perceived limitations

- encourage direct reports to offer new ideas

- empower direct reports to take ownership of their work

The group review does not allow for a deep dive into each team member's profile. Instead, it is designed to familiarize all of them with what the Striver Quotient® Assessment measures. The group review sets up one-on-one meetings that I conduct with each team member at a later time.

I start the group review by making the following points. In the process, I occasionally go back to the whiteboard to reference the terms presented on the matrix:

1. The SQ evaluates one's willingness to compete, to strive together in four relationships: Self, Team, Boss, and Direct Reports.

2. People are evaluated on a scale of zero to one hundred for each attribute. From left to right, along the continuum from zero to one hundred, there are three categories: Cooperative, Collaborative, and Competitive.

3. You are probably wondering what the problem with cooperation is, and why it is on the low end of the continuum. In the initial stages of the design process, I reached out to leaders in different industries and asked them what they thought should be on the low end of the continuum if "Competitive" is on the high end of the continuum. Nearly all of them answered "Cooperative." They said that cooperative people prefer to work alone on their part of the project. They want to cooperate. They don't really want a boss either, and if they have one, they want that boss to be flexible. And they certainly do not want direct reports under them. In general, they do not want to be confronted by the hassle of dealing with other people on the job.

4. *Collaborative* means "to work together." It is a very broad, nebulous term that can be used to describe all types of projects, including projects that do not require embracing tension. It is in the middle on this assessment because it's the default mode for people who fear striving together. Collaborative people can deal with some level of uncertainty. In a team setting, they prioritize working on developing harmony. Collaborative people also prefer to have a

boss who sets reachable goals for them, and direct reports who simply say, "Reward me."

5. In a sense, competing is the highest level of collaboration. "Striving together" gives meaning and an edge to "working together." Strivers thrive when challenged to move out of their comfort zones. They want tension in a team environment and they seek out bosses who will push them. In a leadership role, they search for direct reports who say, "Push me."

A Paradigm Shift

Because they will not see their results until after my presentation, team members take the Striver Quotient® Assessment with little or no idea of what it is measuring. They view their profiles after hearing the presentation and discussing the underlying concepts of Strivership, as framed by the matrix. Initially, this can be a riveting experience. For many people, the concept of Strivership is a complete paradigm shift.

In their Relationship to Self, Strivers hold themselves accountable for moving out of their comfort zones to embrace ambiguity. Many young people today are raised to depend on others for motivation, and they have been conditioned to say, "Let's keep each other accountable." Strivers do not depend first and foremost upon others for accountability. They take responsibility for their own actions.

Building a competitive Relationship to Team requires teammates to push one another out of their comfort zones. In this environment, tension will inevitably arise, but when they leave the field or the meeting room, they must support each other unconditionally. I have had teams whose primary goal was to get along, and we always underachieved. When the "respect" level is lower than the "like" level, the respect level never catches up. But when the respect level starts out higher than the like level, the like level always catches up. The ultimate team bonding experience results from striving together.

All relationships must be based on respect. In addition to challenging and supporting your teammates, you must be committed to communicating with them if serious issues arise. You must communicate primarily because it is your responsibility to continue building your relationship with other teammates. Failure to clear the air creates distraction. If allowed to fester, the two people involved—and eventually the whole team—will suffer. And involving others makes it even worse. Triangulation is a disease that can cripple a team.

Leaders' efforts to intercede can severely exacerbate this. If you're a leader and a teammate complains to you about another teammate, you should send the individual to the source, rather than attempting to mediate. Make it clear that you are willing to help with how to approach their teammate, but you will not inject yourself into the conflict.

Almost every team I've assessed in sports and business scores very high in "willingness to support teammates," but low or mediocre in both "willingness to challenge teammates" and "willingness to communicate with teammates." "Support your teammates" is the clarion call for leaders of winning teams. But in this scenario, the support offered inevitably loses meaning and becomes superficial; support is easy to fake. People who are not committed to pushing their teammates and communicating with them are not supporting them. Without respect, support is meaningless.

When it comes to their Relationship to Boss, most people seek to be motivated. They want to be told what to do. Strivers, however, are self-motivated. You can manage people who are not self-motivated, but you cannot lead them. If we're going somewhere we've never been before, and you are in a leadership position, you must be led. As with Relationship to Team, most groups I've assessed score high in "willingness to support," but low in both "willingness to challenge" and "willingness to communicate." People who are not committed to communicating with their boss when issues arise are not meaningfully supporting their boss.

My First Big Test

In the fall of 2014, I received a call from an old friend and rival, Geoff Macdonald, the tennis coach at Vanderbilt University. Geoff wanted my help. He had already become a very successful coach, having led his Commodores to appearances in the NCAA Final Four and the Finals.

Initially, I wondered why Geoff was calling me for help. He told me that he needed some juice after two very difficult years. He went on to say that he now had a great group of athletes who were, in his estimation, capable of becoming great competitors. The team's preseason ranking was number twelve nationally. In the sport of college tennis, the odds of a team ranked outside of the top four winning the NCAA Title are slim. There were no blue-chip recruits on Vanderbilt's roster, but Geoff believed that his team had enormous untapped potential, and he wanted me to help.

This was my first consulting job with a sports client, so I had the Vanderbilt athletes and coaches take the Striver Quotient® Assessment. Then I traveled to campus to deliver my presentation and conduct profile reviews for the team as a group, as well as one-on-one sessions with team leaders. I also observed practices and met with the team members after each one to ask them questions about how they'd responded to situations that Geoff and his assistant, Aleke Tsoubanas, had put them in. As with business leaders, I was there to tee up Geoff's people for him, not coach them. My goal was to help him better leverage the leadership skills he'd already developed.

Over the next eight months, Geoff and I talked regularly on the phone. His athletes showed steady improvement in practice. They were becoming competitors. However, this improvement did not manifest in dual match results in the short term. The team suffered through tough losses in the early going. Geoff had put together a brutal dual match schedule; two months into the season, Vanderbilt's record was four to four. At this point in most people's minds there was no reason to think the Commodores would be title contenders at the NCAA Championships.

With most sports team practices, intensity tends to fade as the regular season progresses, but Geoff's athletes never took their foot off the pedal. They pushed each other relentlessly in practice. When personal issues came up, they demonstrated respect for each other by communicating directly and in a timely manner.

Vanderbilt ended the 2015 regular season with a flourish by winning the SEC championship. The team entered the NCAA Championship tournament seeded fourth, but despite a strong regular season finish, the team was still a long shot to win the national title. But they would not be denied. They defeated an ultratalented Florida team in the quarterfinals, then upset USC and UCLA, two teams full of blue-chip recruits, to win the title and complete their magical season.

Geoff gave me far too much credit for Vanderbilt's success when he was interviewed about the team's amazing run, but that success and Geoff's comments served to jump-start my business. The demand for my services skyrocketed. But I was not going to fall into the same trap I'd fallen into when I arrived at Texas as a twentysomething; I wasn't going to become an Arriver again. I understood that I had played a small role in Vanderbilt's success, but that I'd also learned at least as much from Geoff as I'd imparted to him.

My ability to use the Striver Quotient® Assessment Tool as a catalyst for my consulting was elevated to a new level during my time working with Geoff and his team. It became clear during this experience that what sets my approach apart from other leadership coaches' is that I did not offer a quick fix. I was providing leaders with a framework for building championship teams by modeling and cultivating Striver Attributes.

SQ Actionability

Companies and sports teams invest heavily in identifying and attracting top performers. They spend considerable time, money, and resources toward this end. The problem is that most of these organizations are not looking for the right qualities in people. This is because most assessment tools evaluate personality traits in search of "personality fits." There are more than two thousand personality tests on the market now, with the Myers-Briggs Type Indicator (MBTI) being one of the oldest and most popular. Results from the MBTI assign one of sixteen personality types to people who take it.

Results from personality assessments can be detrimental to businesses and sports teams because they provide labels that are often transitory. More than half of people who take the MBTI twice receive a different result, and most people fall in between binaries like "introverted" and "extroverted." Their personalities change depending on the circumstances they face.

I once had lunch with a friend who is a highly successful corporate executive, and we started talking about personality assessments. He told me that he had recently taken the Myers-Briggs test and that he was not an "ESTJ," a label that is most often associated with extraversion and is described as the personality type of a leader. In fact, he was the opposite—an "INFP," a label most often associated with introversion. According to Myers-Briggs, my friend is not an ideal leader.

However, many of the leaders who have revolutionized the business world are not extroverts. In fact, the one thing Mark Zuckerberg, Elon Musk, and Jeff Bezos all have in common is that they're introverts.

Introverts often make better leaders because they listen. My friend is certainly a leader, but one of the most trusted personality tests says he's not. It is difficult to connect results from personality assessments to meaningful action.

> *A personality assessment measures discrete personality traits and tells you **who** you are. The Striver Quotient® Assessment indicates **where** you are by evaluating performance attributes.*

As I stated before, a personality assessment measures discrete personality traits and tells you *who* you are. The Striver Quotient® Assessment indicates *where* you are by evaluating performance attributes. Results from the Striver Quotient® Assessment Tool do not provide labels; an SQ Profile does not include numbers, nor does it designate you as a Striver or Arriver. It tells you where you are on the continuum at this point in time, based entirely on your current situation. If you're going through particularly challenging times, your scores could be lower than they would be at other times.

What makes the SQ revolutionary is that the results are truly actionable. By asking you questions related to where you are with respect to each attribute, you can choose to take action. If your SQ Profile indicates that you are resisting the desire to move out of your comfort zone, I will ask what's holding you back. Are you hesitant to act because you are not sure of the consequences? Is there something you know you should try that would make you better? And if so, what's holding you back? These types of questions challenge clients to ask themselves how badly they want to perform at a higher level.

On a typical SQ Profile, all four relationships and the attributes within them are linked. For example, in Relationship to Self, if your score on attribute number one indicates an unwillingness to initiate moving out of your comfort zone, then you may be holding back because of your boss relationship. Maybe your boss wants you to keep your head down, stay in your lane, and just do your job. He wants to be the source of all new ideas, and feels threatened when he's not. If repeated attempts to communicate with your boss are not productive, then your only choices are to stay and suffer, or find a new boss.

In Relationship to Team, you could resist moving out of your comfort zone if your boss tolerates triangulation. Instead of communicating directly with the source when issues arise with a teammate, you're allowed take the easy way out and involve a third party. Consequently, your problem with the source festers and tensions mount. Lack of direct communication exacerbated by triangulation can suck the life out of a team.

In addition to individual SQ Profiles, I also generate an SQ Team Profile. It displays results for the team as a group, with scores for each of the sixteen Striver Attributes. This profile can be displayed with or without the boss. It is possible for bosses to gain valuable feedback by comparing their profile with their team's profile.

One of my first clients was the CEO of a public relations company. She was extraordinarily bright and had a sunny, upbeat personality. She was very well-liked by her team, so when I first saw the team's Relationship to Boss attribute number three, I was surprised. It indicated a resistance on the part of her direct reports to communicate with her when issues arise. When we met to look at her team's profile, she immediately noticed the score.

"How is that possible?" she wondered. "Why do my people hesitate to communicate with me when things get tough?"

I told her to look at her Relationship to Direct Reports attribute number four, her willingness to empower and trust people to do their best. Her score indicated that she did not really trust her people. She was a (likeable) micromanager seeking compliance.

Before I'd even finished telling her this, she interjected. "You know John, our social media director? He's brilliant, but I feel like I can't let go."

I said, "The next time you feel like you can't let go, just let go."

That was a real "aha" moment for her. She relaxed her grip and let go, and her timing was perfect. During South by Southwest the following week, John put out a series of social media posts designed to promote one of the firm's new clients. John's posts vaulted the client from relative obscurity to become a viral sensation.

A Striver had been unleashed.

PART TWO

BUILDING
CHAMPIONSHIP TEAMS

CHAPTER SIX

LEAD BY BEING LED

But of a good leader, when his work is done, his aim fulfilled, they will say, "We did this ourselves."

—Lao-Tzu

When I started my business, one of the first things I did was head to the local Barnes & Noble store. I had never read a leadership book in my life, but now that helping people with leadership was going to be my business, I figured I should find out what the "experts" were saying. I asked the person behind the counter where I could find leadership books and was told they were in the management section. Something didn't seem right.

"No. I'm sorry. I'm looking for *leadership* books."

The clerk reiterated that I could find them in the management section.

But why was leadership being treating as a subset of management? If anything, it's management that is a subset of leadership. Barnes & Noble's categorization reflects a common attitude about management and leadership, namely that they are one and the same. The truth is management and leadership are distinctly different and not interchangeable.

Management is a science. Leadership is an art. Management is about process, efficiency, and strategy. Leadership is about something much more intangible.

The science of management was developed in the early 1900s during the Industrial Revolution by Frederick Taylor, who sought to create efficiency through production management. His concept of mass production transformed the industrial world. The science of management was adopted with an almost religious zeal by the corporate world.

Management is crucially important. If your organization's processes are not operating efficiently and you don't have a well-thought-out strategy for execution, you will sink. Good management is imperative. However, management, with proper oversight, can be delegated. Leadership cannot be delegated.

Those in leadership roles who manage seek to control people the same way they seek to control process. All ideas flow in one direction. Managers often possess a strong ego, but they lack empathy. Managers know where they want their organization to go and are set on what it's going to look like when all is said and done. They also feel compelled to micromanage their people during every step along the way. Any attempts to lead from someone who is below them on the flow chart are viewed as threats or insubordination. Granting autonomy in the interest of seeking the best possible outcome is not an option. This would require demonstrating empathy, which would force them outside their comfort zone. Managers are not interested in the best possible outcome. They are interested in achieving an outcome that reflects best on them.

Leaders possess strong ego drive, but also the capacity to demonstrate empathy. They intentionally put themselves in the shoes of their people because they seek to be led by them. Leaders lay out a strong vision. They know where they want their organization to go, but they don't attempt to determine exactly what it's going to look like when they reach the destination. And to achieve the best possible outcome, they want their people to *lead them* there. Leaders lead by being led. When the job is done, leaders want their people to say, "We did this!"

Leaders thrive when challenged to move outside their comfort zones. They make themselves vulnerable by engaging their people, pushing them to set high, seemingly unreachable goals. Then they inspire their people to achieve beyond expectations by challenging them to stretch beyond their perceived limitations. And just as they challenge their people, leaders welcome and respond to being challenged by them in return. Leaders want to lead people who embrace Strivership. Essentially, they want to lead a group of people who are themselves leading by example.

Inspiring someone to achieve beyond expectations is very different from mastering the science of management. You can *become* a manager because management can be taught. Leadership, on the other hand, must be cultivated over time. Those who truly aspire to be leaders

> *You can become a manager because management can be taught. Leadership, on the other hand, must be cultivated over time.*

never view themselves as complete. They are forever immersed in the process of *becoming* a leader.

As my friend and prominent business leader Tony Capasso has said, "Managing is the easy part. It can be delegated. Leading is the hard part. It requires courage."

Society is starved for leadership now because we don't dream anymore. Leaders are mindful of the *actual*, but they are driven by what is *possible*. We once embodied this mind-set as a country. In 1962, JFK implored us to dream when he said, "We choose to go to the moon in this decade and do the other things, not because they are easy, *but because they are hard.*" Kennedy was modeling what great leaders do: they are comfortable being uncomfortable. They inspire and empower their people to move from *the actual* to *the possible*. In effect, JFK was pushing Americans to stretch themselves, moving beyond simply working together to strive together.

As I stood before the management section at Barnes & Noble, I found myself asking, what did famous American leaders like George Washington or Abraham Lincoln do without these "leadership" books? Those guys didn't have a formula to follow for effective leadership. I also found myself wondering, with all the how-to leadership books we have today, why do there seem to be fewer leaders than ever before?

Historic Leadership

When it comes to US history, perhaps no figure looms larger than George Washington. The father of our nation has been dubbed by historians "the indispensable man,"[11] meaning that without him, the US would have never won its independence.

By all accounts, Washington was a great leader. When the Continental Congress needed someone to lead the new army, leaders looked to Washington. When his troops were in the fog of war, they would look to Washington and see he was right there with them. Described as the last man to retreat, Washington earned tremendous loyalty and respect from his men. When the new country sought to ratify a controversial new Constitution, it trusted only Washington to preside over the process. And when it came time for that new nation to choose its first president, the choice was obvious.

Washington wasn't born a leader, however, nor was he taught how to lead. For Washington, leadership was modeled by historic figures, his brothers, and his superiors. Over time, the seeds of leadership were planted as he studied and learned from these role models. He read about the lives of great Roman leaders like Cincinnatus and Cicero. In his life, he studied and absorbed lessons from the leaders around him—some modeled what to do, others modeled what *not* to do.

As a young man, Washington enlisted in the British Army. It was in that capacity, leading an attack on French forces at Jumonville Glen, that Washington created the spark that would ignite the French and Indian War—a war that would make him a hero.

During the French and Indian War, Washington served under General Edward Braddock, who became a role model for Washington's development as a leader. Braddock was narrow-minded and rigidly traditional. He believed in the rules of traditional British warfare and tactics. Washington found these tactics to be antiquated

---

11   James Flexner, *Washington: The Indispensable Man* (New York: Back Bay Books, 1994).

and ineffective, especially when battling Native Americans, whose fighting tactics were anything but conventional. Braddock dismissed Washington's advice, and faced humiliating defeat at the battle at Fort Duquesne as a result.

Braddock's example was not all bad, though. He was adept at politics and a masterful organizer. Washington learned how to play the game of politics as a general—something that would prove valuable to him when he later led the Continental Army.

Washington embraced Strivership. He was an ambitious man, always pursuing larger-than-life goals. He was always reaching beyond his grasp. He thrived when challenged to live outside of his comfort zone. When Washington led the expedition that would trigger the French and Indian War, it was his first time leading an expedition. When the Continental Congress wanted someone to lead an army against England—the strongest empire the world had ever known—in the Revolutionary War, Washington didn't blink. When the musket balls were flying in the heat of battle, Washington was there in the thick of it. When it came time to lead a new country mired in uncertainty, Washington was there to provide leadership.

And yet for all of his successes, Washington was a man of many failures. Nearly every battle he fought in 1776, the opening year of America's war for independence, ended in defeat and retreat. Time after time, Washington suffered defeat and humiliation. His army was poorly funded, undersupplied, and struggling to hold onto volunteers. Soldiers marched for miles barefoot in the snow and ice. When it comes to being out of your comfort zone, harsh winters at Valley Forge are probably near the top of the list.

Throughout all the doubt and uncertainty, Washington maintained his resolve. He continued to lead and in doing so, cultivated Strivership in his ranks. He was America's first leader and has since become an archetype for leadership. He showed perseverance and resolve in a time of national crisis.

Just imagine how Washington had to move outside his comfort zone to accept the position of general in the new Continental Army. Defeating the most powerful military the world had ever known would require demonstrating two key Striver Attributes: finding unconventional solutions to extremely vexing problems and persevering through the inevitable setbacks he faced while tackling those problems.

Despite the harsh conditions, he constantly circulated among his troops to model these attributes. He adjusted his tactics when confronted with the British, who had a huge, well-trained standing army. Instead of facing them in open combat he resorted to what we now call guerilla warfare. He refused to reside in lavish housing, unlike most generals of the time. He purposely arranged to have modest living quarters built. He was America's first leader and has since become an archetype for leadership.

Abraham Lincoln is another president who, like Washington, also led the country through a time of great crisis. Lincoln led during an era when the country had never been so divided. His convictions alone were enough to spark a civil war upon his election. So began a time of extraordinary challenges that called for an extraordinary leader. Lincoln was that leader.

Lincoln, like Washington, was a student of classical history. Whereas Washington found inspiration from Roman leaders, Lincoln studied Greek figures such as Markos Botsaris, a heroic captain during Greece's war for independence, and ancient mythological figures such as Achilles and Theseus. Lincoln also took an interest in reading about Washington and the other founding fathers.

While Washington learned leadership in the field, Lincoln developed his skill in the courtroom. Under the tutelage of legal master and statesman Henry Clay, Lincoln learned the law and how to effectively communicate to groups through oratory—a skill that would bring him national attention when he famously debated Senator Stephen Douglas over the issue of slavery.

When Lincoln was running for president, the prospect of a civil war loomed large on the horizon. By opposing the expansion of slavery, Lincoln knew he could be fracturing the country—but his convictions would not allow him to concede on the issue.

Can you imagine the discomfort of doing what you knew was morally right, but knowing that it would cause a war of unimaginable destruction? It is fair to say that Lincoln lived in a constant state of discomfort from the time he was elected until his death just five years later. However, through it all, he remained a steady and principled leader.

Washington and Lincoln both immersed themselves in situations requiring continual problem solving during extraordinarily difficult times. Role models and real-world experience cultivated leadership skills in them over time. Yes, they read extensively; but they didn't read how-to manuals on leadership. They read *about* great leaders and used them as models. Cincinnatus didn't write a memoir on how to lead that Washington could follow. Washington used him as an archetypal role model. The same was true for Lincoln as he studied Clay, Washington, and others. In both men, these role models planted seeds that were cultivated over time through experience. Both men thrived in immensely difficult situations—and their leadership shaped history.

Where Are Our Leaders Today?

When looking back at leaders like Washington and Lincoln, it's hard to imagine that kind of leader emerging today. Our economy has never been larger, there have never been more successful small businesses, and technology is opening doors to whole new industries. You would assume, in this modern age, that we would have more leaders than ever.

The remarkable world of innovation we live in was certainly created by exceptional leaders. People like Steve Jobs led us into a new world of possibility and brought us all closer together. What is it about leaders like Jobs that makes them successful? I think it's the same factors that made Washington and Lincoln great leaders. They were Strivers who thrived in extremely uncomfortable situations where they persevered to find innovative ways to solve seemingly intractable problems.

Which is not to say that leaders are invincible, impervious, or even always resilient. Steve Jobs was once pushed out of his own company. Washington faced a rebellion from angry farmers during his first term. Lincoln lost elections, failed in business, and faced constant opposition from enemies and allies alike during his presidency. All three men had to struggle against defeatist attitudes, even depression, at times. Leaders, for all their strengths, are human. They all ride the Striver-Arriver roller coaster. An embrace of Strivership requires a willingness to be persistent when confronted with seemingly intractable problems in the most adverse circumstances.

If modern leaders really want to learn about leadership, they'll walk past the management section at Barnes & Noble and over to the US history or biographies section. Study historic leaders—the longer they've been dead, the better. Because it's hard to have empathy and be free of any biases if you're reading about leaders who lived in your time. It's too fresh, likely polarized, and there's no historic perspective yet.

The problem with leadership today is there are too many people who think leading is managing. Managers effectively treat their people as if they were software (and sometimes use software to "manage" them!). Managers do not spend much time building relationships with their direct reports. And all direction comes from the top. Managers expect their direct reports to work toward their clearly defined objectives. Leaders embrace a spirit of Strivership, dispelling the myth that leadership starts with the leader. They build strong relationships with their direct reports by inspiring and empowering them to stretch beyond their perceived limitations. Leaders lead by being led.

Today, large segments of the US workforce are disengaged at work, and the vast majority of those people are disengaged because of their boss. That's a leadership problem. Part of that problem is too many consider leading a type of management. As I said before, management is very important. There are many terrific books written on management, and the science of management is always improving. But managers do not lead. They don't engage their people by challenging them.

The true nature of competition seems to be falling more and more out of favor. Strivers are being replaced in leadership positions by Arrivers, who want things to function smoothly so that they look good and everyone is happy. Strivers are wired to tackle the thorny issues that require moving out of their comfort zone. The more Strivers we have, the more challenges as a society we can overcome.

Cultivating a Spirit of Strivership

One of the parents I met while I was at Trinity Episcopal School was Jimmy Treybig, an influential figure during the early years of Silicon Valley. Jimmy started working at Hewlett-Packard before going on to found Tandem Computers. He has a great humility about him. He is very wealthy, but you would never guess it judging by the way he comes across.

I remember being at a basketball game with him, and Michael Dell was in the stands. Dell had a lot of people crowding around him. Jimmy was not attracting attention. He had an unassuming nature and appearance that belied his status as a tech pioneer. Dell noticed Jimmy, left his admirers, walked right over to sit next to Jimmy, and became engrossed in conversation. That's how important Jimmy is to the people who understand the value of the wisdom he possesses.

When I first started my business and was beginning to design my assessment, Jimmy and I would meet and he would make seemingly random suggestions like, "You need to look at match.com. You could learn about the algorithms they use to help build your assessment tool."

Like most people in the tech industry, Jimmy was highly intelligent. But what separated him was his ability to synthesize—to connect dots. He was a brilliant engineer with a creative mind.

Jimmy had always been intrigued by what I was trying to accomplish at Trinity. During one of our meetings he made a comment that initially puzzled me. He said that I had developed a "spirit" at Trinity.

I remember feeling underwhelmed by this comment initially.

I was already being sucked in by the you-better-promote-yourself mentality, so my first thought was, "Why couldn't he have called me a 'leadership guru' or 'CEO whisperer'—something a bit more attention-grabbing?" Then I took a step back and said to myself, "The 'wow' factor of a mantra like 'leadership guru' or 'CEO whisperer' is typically phony and used for effect. Jimmy's not enamored with smoke and mirrors. But what did he mean by 'spirit'?"

Then it clicked. Jimmy had seen right through the window dressing to the heart of what I do. He was essentially saying that what I had developed at the school was much more than a defined, prescribed culture; it was a feeling—a *spirit*.

Jimmy's observation really rings true, and I think he hit on the reason why we don't have more exceptional leaders today. Most companies understand the importance of culture and, as such, most companies promote their culture. What they fail to do is cultivate a spirit. What does that mean?

Managers hold up a list of core values or attributes and say, "Hey, team, these attributes are what I'm about. This is what our company is about. We will talk about these attributes in our biweekly meetings, and they will be displayed on the wall of every room in this building."

The problem with promoting and prescribing values or attributes is that this approach keeps them in the abstract. It becomes a check-the-box exercise. I could tell my team, "Let's be problem solvers!" before a meeting and "Way to be resilient!" after it's over, but I would not be attaching those comments to any actions. All you're doing when you promote a culture is sending out signals for what you would like your people to emulate. You're providing them with a CliffsNotes version of what it takes to become an A-player. Then, once a year, in a formal performance review, you reduce all of your people to a number by giving each of them a grade.

Managers promote. Leaders cultivate. What does that look like?

Cultivating involves recognizing when a person exhibits competitive attributes and nurturing them in the moment. You are not instructing them with a direct message, "This is how you need to solve this problem." And you don't reduce them to a number by grading their performance. You are capturing a moment in real time when they are compelled to move out of their comfort zone to solve a difficult problem and responding with reinforcement—in the form of an observation or a question—that is related to their actions.

Pretend for a moment that I am your boss, and you have just knocked a project out of the park and exceeded all expectations. If I were a promoter, I would schedule an appointment for a formal meeting with you at my office and say something like, "Great job on that project! I am giving you a four out of five for problem solving this week!" That is a general statement that does not capture an actual moment when problem solving is happening. A sweeping acknowledgment that ends with a numerical rating sends a message that all you care about is results.

If I was a cultivator, I would drop by your office unexpectedly during a walk-around, poke my head in, and say, "Hey, you did a great job on that project." Then I would step inside the office and follow up with, "How did you solve that problem? You must have had to come at it in several different ways! I bet it was stressful trying to find the right solution. Tell me about it." By taking this approach I am putting myself in your shoes and showing that I understand what it took for you to do what you did. And by doing so, I'm demonstrating appreciation for specific Striver Attributes, planting seeds that convey my belief in your ability to overachieve. I am inspiring you to stretch beyond what you perceive to be your limitations, which can lead to unimaginable results.

As a cultivator, I am getting into your head and really taking the time to consider what this achievement took. In doing so, I am highlighting what attributes made you successful and thus encouraging you to use those attributes more. If I just tell you, "That's good work. Nicely done," you will feel good. However, if I tell you, "Wow, I can't believe you got this done. You must have had to break down every door in this building!" you're going to be inspired to continue to stretch yourself.

This approach cultivates Striver Attributes like problem solving and resilience without even saying those words. You are motivating people in a way that also challenges them. The result? A spirit of Strivership!

A Leader Is Always Becoming a Leader

I generally work with two types of leaders. One is the individual who is already leading in some capacity, but wants to get better. The other is typically a young, emerging leader who is starting from scratch and wants to learn. Whether they are experienced or green behind the ears doesn't matter. What does matter is they must possess two key traits: strong ego drive and empathy. In many young, emerging leaders these traits may lie dormant, waiting to be drawn out.

It's a bit of a contradiction: ego drive and empathy are, after all, typically viewed as conflicting. Ego drive involves your vision and sense of purpose for the organization. Leaders know where they would like to see their organization go and why. Ego drive keeps them motivated and moving forward during difficult times. That ego feeds a need to acquire more skills and continually improve to confront and learn from setbacks along the way.

However, to effectively lead others on this path, leaders will also need to employ real empathy. They exhibit empathy by demonstrating their willingness to put themselves in their people's shoes.

However contradictory it may seem, good leaders need to have both ego and empathy.

Leaders know where they want to go, but they don't prescribe *how* they're going to get there. Although leaders make final decisions, they ensure that their people are engaged in the process. They set the destination by saying, "This is where we are heading," but they make sure everybody is involved in getting there. "What do you think? How can we handle this problem if it arises?" Involving others and really considering what they have to say requires empathy.

Leaders with empathy, but no ego, will not be able to effectively lead. They will typically struggle to provide direction and make decisions. Their people will be reluctant to become fully engaged in the process. Most people are not eager to board a rudderless ship.

Leaders with ego but no empathy are managers. Everything is about them. All ideas must come from the top, or at least have the appearance of having originated there. Managers have no interest in involving their people in the decision-making process in any meaningful way.

When I am considering working with people in a leadership position, a red flag pops up when they tell me their leadership team needs training, omitting themselves. For my process to work, leadership must start at the top, and *everyone* must be involved and willing to make changes. *A leader is always becoming a leader.*

CHAPTER SEVEN

BUILDING CHAMPIONSHIP COMPANIES

The mission of Southwest Airlines is dedication to the highest quality of customer service delivered with a sense of warmth, friendliness, individual pride, and company spirit.

—Southwest Airlines

What is *company spirit?* Spirit evokes thoughts of life. There's a powerful mystique about it. A spirit is something intangible that cannot be measured. When a company has spirit, it's evident, and Southwest Airlines has it. When I step onto a Southwest flight, it really *feels* different.

Once, on a road trip to the East Coast, I got stuck in a howling snowstorm in the Baltimore airport. My connecting flight was cancelled, as often happens in these situations. Chaos ensued. The mad scramble for alternative arrangements was on.

I quickly found my spot in the long line that had formed to talk to Belinda, the gate agent on duty, about changing my flight. You could feel the tension in the air. Most gate agents dread this type of situation because they know they're going to have to deal with difficult people. There were three people who fit that description in front of me, ready to confront Belinda. I had a ringside seat. I'll call them Terrible Tom, Earl the Expert, and Panicky Polly.

When Terrible Tom got to Belinda, he simply lost it! However, she defused him beautifully. Soon his blood pressure was close to normal. Next, Earl the Expert stepped up. He was supremely confident that he knew more about the possible options than anyone at Southwest. He immediately engaged Belinda in debate. She listened to his pushback, then assertively but calmly made his options clear to him.

Then Polly's turn came. She had a legitimate emergency, wanting to get home to see her mother who was on her deathbed. She was travelling on a free ticket, which the computer was not handling well. This made Belinda's task even more difficult. Then, to further complicate things, Belinda received a call on her cell phone from her child's day-care center. Her child was sick and needed to be picked up. I could see the stress on Belinda's face. She was a single mom confronted with desperate travelers and a sick child.

Then another agent named Curtis came to the rescue, coming off his break early to relieve Belinda. He actually shuffled to the counter and chirped in an upbeat tone, "What's goin' on Belinda?" Then he stared at the computer screen and said with a smile, "Oh, nothing we can't handle." He picked up right where she had left off.

When I finally boarded my flight, sandwich in hand, the flight attendant greeted me with a big smile and said, "Oh, are we having a picnic today?"

Other airlines put the words *customer service* in their missions, but they amount to nothing more than statements designed to serve the marketing strategy, not customers. With these other airlines, I feel like a number, not a person.

Southwest Airlines is a championship company. Its people exude a spirit of Strivership. They possess a mystique that cannot be explained, which can be intimidating to competitors. Southwest's mission statement not only uses the word *spirit*, it oozes spirit.

The other airlines are winning companies with mission statements like Delta's: *"We—Delta's employees, customers, and community partners—together form a force for positive local and global change, dedicated to bettering standards of living and the environment where we and our customers live and work."*

This is a classic check-the-box mission statement; elegantly composed and chock-full of buzzwords. But what does it mean? How does this statement in any way resonate with the customer?

Winning companies are built from the outside in. They are obsessed with results. Making a profit is their only concern, and success must always be within their grasp. They don't compete—they compare. Every step of the way is benchmarked to assess progress toward achieving a reachable profit goal. This approach is not sustainable because obsessive attention to results causes a gradual lowering of the bar.

When striving together is top of mind, great results follow. How has Southwest fared? How about forty-five consecutive years of profitability? During those forty-five years, some of the carrier's competitors have gone out of business, and all of the others have endured bankruptcies, mergers, downsizing, or all of the above. Southwest hasn't ever fired anyone.[12]

"Get a win!" is the rallying cry for winning companies. These companies could succeed in the Industrial Age because the solutions to the problems they confronted were straightforward and, with hard work, clearly achievable. You could make a plan and execute on it to deliver a product that fulfilled an established consumer need. And sales of that product could continue to bring in revenue for years.

Now, in the Age of Innovation, wins are a lot harder to come by in the corporate world. Winning companies struggle because product cycles have been drastically shortened. When asked about the biggest challenge they face, CEOs no longer respond with reliable go-to responses like "better *management* discipline." Instead, they now say things like "coping with change."

> *Mantras like "work hard" and "working together" sufficed during the Industrial Age because collaboration—"working together"—drives efficiency, which was the key to success in a linear and predictable economy.*

In the current economy of rapid change, the winners are companies that are committed to building championship teams. Mantras like "work hard" and "working together" sufficed during the Industrial Age because collaboration—"working together"—drives efficiency, which was the key to success in a linear and predictable economy.

But in the Age of Innovation, striving together is required

---

12   Jim Schleckser, "Why Southwest Has Been Profitable 45 Years in a Row," *Inc.*, August 28, 2018, https://www.inc.com/jim-schleckser/why-southwest-has-been-profitable-45-years-in-a-row.html.

because productivity is the key driver. Only Strivers thrive in this new economy in which last year's products are last year's dollars. Strivers respond proactively to the constant pressure to innovate. Their eyes light up when they're told it's time to go back to the drawing board. It's their SQ—their ability to adapt to change—that is now the real game changer. Strivers from Mediocre State University with sub-3.0 GPAs typically outperform A-players brandishing high IQs and Ivy League pedigrees. A company full of thoroughbreds groomed for success had better plan for high attrition. That company's success will be short-lived when its steps into the arena with a company full of broncos who have learned to run straight.

A Case Study in Strivership

Any effort to build championship teams in business must start at the top with the leader and emanate throughout the entire organization. Managers typically insist their direct reports always take direction from above. Leaders lead by being led. They inspire and empower direct reports to become proactive participants in both decision-making and execution.

One such leader is Tony Capasso, a highly respected executive in the burgeoning Austin tech industry. Tony's path to becoming a prominent leader in business began in the sports world. He arrived at the University of Texas as an assistant coach for the women's soccer team near the end of my coaching career. He had just graduated from Notre Dame, where he had been an All-American soccer player. Tony modeled Striver Attributes the minute he stepped on campus. He had an engaging personality and a relentless desire to get better. He and I had long discussions about coaching, and would often get together to review videos.

Tony challenged me to support my philosophy of coaching and offered keen, well-thought-out insights. I remember thinking, "This kid is going to be something special." Tony channeled Strivership in all relationships. In Relationship to Self, he eagerly moved out of his comfort zone to create training programs that really made a difference. He refused to simply replicate programs that other coaches were using. Instead, he combined what he learned from others with his own ideas to create his best practices. In Relationship to Team, he did not hesitate to challenge coworkers, but at the same time he supported them. What happened in the meeting room stayed in the meeting room.

After more than five years at Texas, Tony decided to leave coaching. It took him a few years and a couple of career detours before he found an industry where he could once again truly channel Strivership.

Tony eventually applied for a sales position with Bazaarvoice, a new company that had fewer than fifty employees at the time. Bazaarvoice provided software that would allow companies to compete with Amazon by enabling user review technology on their websites. The company was founded by a brilliant entrepreneur named Brett Hurt. A key part of the interview process for a sales position was an audition. Tony was given forty-eight hours to prepare a presentation for a panel of executives, demonstrating how he would sell their software. Tony had no experience with software sales platforms, and was given the feedback that his presentation was on the edge of a pass. He would need to convince Brett that Bazaarvoice should hire him.

Brett looked at Tony's resume and said, "Given your lack of experience, I would never have hired you in my last five companies. But, I can see you have leadership ability and an interesting background."

Tony went on to acknowledge his lack of experience but reminded Brett that he had succeeded at nearly every challenge presented him to date and said, "If you hire me I will learn about software and outperform everyone in this company."

Brett said, "OK, but this is going to go one of two ways. You will either be wildly successful or fail completely. There will be no in between."

Tony quickly learned about the enterprise software business and went on to become one of the top producers at Bazaarvoice. Tony was wildly successful, and not because he thought of himself as an A-player. He did not view himself as a "complete package." Instead, he embraced Strivership by viewing himself as incomplete. His willingness to enter into and succeed in an industry completely foreign to him demonstrated how he thrives when challenged to move out of his comfort zone.

It did not take long before he was asked to lead a sales team. Bazaarvoice became a billion-dollar company with more than nine hundred employees globally. The word got out that Tony was a big part of that explosive growth. After six years with the company, he was recruited to be VP of sales at Civitas Learning—another software start-up. Civitas quickly became one of the fastest growing companies in the US and the leader in retention software for higher education. Eventually, he was promoted to chief revenue officer at Civitas. Today he is the chief revenue officer at another early-stage company called YouEarnedIt in Austin.

Tony's experience going through the hiring process at Bazaarvoice taught him valuable lessons about how not to go about recruiting. He made several outside-the-box hires. Recruits did not have to be proven software sales experts, because he was not looking for A-players. He searched for people who constantly sought to reach beyond their grasp. But Tony knew that the process of building a championship company—a company that overachieves—does not start with recruiting. He understood that championship teams are built when companies embrace Strivership. Instead of simply focusing on competing externally with the Competition, Tony cultivated internal competition so his team members were ready for anything that the Competition could throw at them. And his actions were contagious! Soon members of his leadership team began cultivating Strivership in their own direct reports. Tony's focus on inspiring his people to stretch enabled his team to consistently achieve beyond expectations.

Cultivating Striver Attributes

I help executives like Tony Capasso build championship teams by providing them with a framework to become a better leader in a way that reflects their own inner voice and personality. The building process is often a paradigm shift for everyone involved. Most people in leadership positions are accustomed to building from the outside in. It's all about "how things look." They promote a culture by essentially marketing the company's values to their own people.

Let's say, for example, that your company's values include promoting Striver Attributes. Your marketing plan would include strategies like

- posting the attributes on walls throughout the company;

- delivering pep talks about the attributes;

- conducting meetings for the purpose of discussing the attributes;

- starting meetings with statements like, "Let's be problem solvers today!";

- ending meetings with statements like, "Way to be resilient!"; and

- rating people with respect to the attributes, such as "I give you a four out of five for resilience this week."

Promoting a culture is a superficial, check-the-box exercise. Display your core values everywhere, occasionally make pronouncements about them, and then once a year sit down with direct reports and give them a grade during the obligatory "performance review." The values are everywhere, but they have no real meaning. No one can explain how these words get translated into action because they are contrived. This is the way most people in leadership positions approach "people matters" in their companies. There is no connection to any action, so the values never become part of the program's DNA.

Another more serious consequence of promoting a culture is that you condition your people to look to you for direction regarding all-important decisions, including the vision of your company. The authors of *Collective Genius: The Art and Practice of Innovation* conducted an extensive study of leaders of innovative companies. They call this "direction-setting leadership." They point out that this type of leadership does not work in the Age of Innovation. Direction-setting leadership, they argue, only works "when the solution to the problem is known and straightforward. But if a problem calls for a truly original response, no one can decide in advance what the response should be. By definition then, leading innovation cannot be about creating and selling a vision to your people and then somehow inspiring them to execute it."[13]

The authors cite Bill Coughran, senior vice president of engineering at Google from 2003 to 2011, as a prime example. His team built Google's "engine room," which powers all Google services. "We were doing work that no one else in the world was doing," he says. "So when a problem happened, we couldn't just go out and buy a solution. We had to create it. The question is how do I build an organization capable of innovating over time?"[14]

The authors concluded that a leader's role in an Age of Innovation is not to "make innovation happen," but rather to "set the stage for it to happen. Coughran knew that the role of a leader of innovation is to create a community that is willing and able to generate ideas."[15]

We have talked extensively about relationships to Self, Team, and Boss. The key to creating an environment that is willing and able to generate new ideas is the nature of the leader's relationship to direct reports. A top-down, direction-setting relationship to direct reports worked when it was possible to simply manage change. In the Age of Innovation, you must articulate a vision that sets the stage for leading change.

Direction-setting executives channel their strong ego drive by issuing instructions, maintaining control so that they can avoid discomfort. Imbuing a spirit is far more challenging. Spirit is a powerful feeling that evolves over time as the attributes become part of your company's DNA. It requires you to move well out of your comfort

13   Linda A. Hill, Greg Brandeau, Emily Truelove, and Kent Lineback, *Collective Genius: The Art and Practice of Leading Innovation* (Boston: Harvard Business Review Press, 2014).

14   Ibid.

15   Ibid.

zone by combining strong ego drive with genuine empathy for your people. A number of steps can build a spirit of Strivership in your company.

Articulate a Purpose-Driven Vision

Your vision should speak to a higher purpose, one that inspires your people to stretch beyond their limitations to achieve beyond expectations. The vision at Southwest Airlines is "to become the world's most loved, most flown, and most profitable airline."

Foster Trusting Relationships with Your Direct Reports

Do this by demonstrating a genuine concern for them as people first and employees second. Build these relationships by making a commitment to learning about your people. Put your views on the shelf and immerse yourself in their world by asking questions. Make this effort during informal moments, not just during scheduled get-togethers. Efforts to foster trusting relationships should be ongoing and never-ending.

Cultivate Striver Attributes by Setting Stretch Goals

You may have certain goals in mind, but keep asking questions until direct reports come up with a goal that requires them to stretch beyond their perceived limitations. In the end the goal must come from them. You will be pleased with the goal, but it's their idea. With this approach to goal-setting, you will be cultivating Striver Attributes in your people simply by taking them through the process.

Cultivate Striver Attributes by Modeling Strivership

Teams are a reflection of their leader. A powerful way to cultivate Striver Attributes is to *model* them. This is not easy to do. When everything around you is chaotic, you must remain calm and clear thinking, even if it's an act. The nonverbal cues that you give off will have a huge impact on your people.

Children pick up far more tendencies from their parents than most parents realize. The same can be said about the people in your charge. The impact of nonverbal cues is often underestimated because it is not immediately discernable. Modeling is a discipline and it is one of the most difficult things to learn during the transition from individual contributor to leader. One minute you're wearing your emotions on your sleeve and the next moment you're having to at least appear to be comfortable with being uncomfortable.

Managers are scoreboard watchers. They model the kind of anxiety that negatively stresses their people. You always know what the score is when you are around them. It is distracting and compromises the ability to focus on competing. Leaders model the kind of anxiety that gets people excited about competing. They exude a love for the battle by modeling Striver Attributes in all relationships.

In Relationship to Self, leaders model the willingness to
- move outside their comfort zone,
- solve difficult problems unconventionally,
- learn new skills,
- persevere through adversity, and
- present an accurate self-image.

In Relationship to Team, leaders model the willingness to

- be assertive and challenge teammates,

- support teammates,

- demonstrate empathy for teammates, and

- communicate directly in a timely manner with the source when issues arise with a teammate.

In Relationship to Boss, leaders model the willingness to

- be assertive by offering their boss new ideas,

- support their boss, and

- communicate directly in a timely manner with their boss if an issue arises.

Cultivate Striver Attributes by Planting the Seeds of Strivership

While pursuing stretch goals, your direct reports will be challenged to stretch beyond their perceived limitations. When this happens, seize opportunities to *plant the seeds of Strivership*. Inspire and empower your people by cultivating the Striver Attributes that you are modeling.

When direct reports demonstrate or fail to demonstrate a Striver Attribute, engage them with questions or observations that address the attribute. For example, let's say that one of your direct reports is successful with a high-risk project that forced her out of her comfort zone. Do you acknowledge the successful outcome? Of course. But then quickly pivot with an observation like, "You really had to put yourself out there to get this done!" Or ask a question like, "How did you create solutions for those two problems you encountered at the end of the process?"

A spirit of Strivership will gradually evolve if you are hypervigilant about capturing moments to intentionally cultivate Striver Attributes in your people. Be creative. Seize every opportunity to cultivate these attributes during walk-arounds and drop-bys, casual bump-ins, individual meetings, team meetings, and interactions with outside entities.

The most impactful way to cultivate Striver Attributes is during informal interactions because they will not come off as staged. Informal interactions during walk-arounds should be the staple of your cultivating efforts. A walk-around should be planned on your part, but appear serendipitous to your direct reports.

Sometimes executives will say to me, "I don't have time to walk around. I'm too busy making sure things run smoothly." I reply, "Make time. It will be time well spent. The work you do during walk-arounds, inspiring and empowering your people to stretch and take ownership of their work, will create far more efficiencies than you could possibly accomplish sitting in your office. The efficiencies won't be reflected on a written report, but you'll know they're happening when the engine starts to really hum." *Casual bump-ins*, a term coined by legendary University of Texas football coach Darrell Royal, are similar in concept to walk-arounds, except that they are serendipitous for both parties. Coach Royal talked about how he was always coaching, even during casual bump-ins with players on campus.

Great leaders are always "on." Here are some examples of questions to pose and observations to make during walk-arounds and casual bump-ins. The attributes being cultivated are in parentheses.

Relationship to Self:

- "You really had to put yourself out there to get this done!" (moving out of comfort zone)

- "Accept this challenge. Jump into the fire. You can do this!" (moving out of comfort zone)

- "This needs to be better! How are you going to make it better? Figure it out. You can do it!" (problem solving)

- "Wow! How the heck did you figure that out? What did you see that I missed?" (problem solving)

- "What obstacles stand in your way and how are you going to overcome them?" (problem solving)

- "Have you approached this problem from every possible angle?" (problem solving)

- "How did you attack that problem?" (problem solving)

- "You never stop learning!" (learning new things)

- "Are you willing to learn this new technique to improve your knowledge base?" (learning new things)

- "You had to overcome so many obstacles to get to this point!" (embrace of failure)

- "Push through this. You can do it." (embrace of failure)

- "What do you really think?!" (authenticity)

- "One thing I respect about you is that what I see is what I get!" (authenticity)

Relationship to Team:

- "How can you challenge your teammates get better?" (challenging teammates)

- "How can your teammates challenge you to get better?" (challenging teammates)

- "I appreciate your willingness to challenge each other." (challenging teammates)

- "Remember, what happens in this meeting room stays in this meeting room." (supporting teammates)

- To the quiet one: "What do you think?" (challenging teammates and demonstrating empathy)

- To the team member who isn't well liked at the time but is a strong contributor: "You were a catalyst today!" (challenging teammates and demonstrating empathy)

- "Jim, if you have an issue with Bill, address it with him directly." (communicating with teammates)

- "Times are tough. When you leave here today, talk to each other. Triangulation is a disease!" (communicating with teammates)

Relationship to Boss:

- "I need pushback." (challenging the boss)

- "I am getting tired of being the motivator! Who's going to step up?" (challenging the boss)

- "What do we need to be doing differently?" (challenging the boss)

- "How do you think the meeting went today? What are your thoughts? How could I have done better?" (communicating with the boss)

- "Do not hesitate to bring problems to me. You will be heard." (communicating with the boss)

- "Thank you for coming in today. Now we're on the same page." (communicating with the boss)

During your cultivating efforts, keep your antennae up to identify emerging leaders. That doesn't necessarily mean identifying people who speak up. Vocal people are not always good leaders. Often, your most impactful leaders are the quiet ones. They operate under the radar because of their tendency to lead with actions more than words.

During individual meetings with direct reports to discuss their goals, focus on cultivating Striver Attributes instead of zeroing in on outcomes or trends toward outcomes. Remember, you want them to stretch, not settle. Challenge direct reports to continue to stretch themselves beyond perceived limitations by evaluating them based primarily on their willingness to strive together. Use questions like:

- "How do you plan to contribute to the pursuit of the team goal?"

- "What can you do to get better? Are you willing to step out of your comfort zone to learn that skill?"

- "How can you help your teammates get better?"

- "Are the lines of direct communication open?"

- "How can your teammates help you get better? How can you be pushed to execute better under pressure?"

- "How can I help you get better?"

Of course, you will want to let your direct reports know where they stand with regard to results, but cultivating Striver Attributes over time will yield far better results! In particular, this approach to individual meetings will cultivate the willingness to move out of one's comfort zone, support teammates, and demonstrate empathy for teammates.

Challenge each direct report to be self-accountable for contributing to a shared commitment to reach the individual and team goals that have been set. As Abraham Lincoln once said, "Always bear in mind that your own resolution to succeed is more important than any other."

You can also cultivate Striver Attributes in your direct reports during team meetings by focusing on asking relentless questions as opposed to telling them what to do. If you have a problem to solve or an issue to address, instead of weighing in heavily right away, ask your direct reports questions to move them toward a resolution. This approach to a team meeting cultivates their willingness to: move out of their comfort zones, problem-solve unconventionally, and challenge teammates—as well as a willingness to challenge you.

Another way to use team meetings to cultivate Striver Attributes is to facilitate sessions where team members determine the essential attributes of a Striver. Again, you would ask questions to get them at least close to a certain place. You could also facilitate sessions to determine, "What should be the expectations of a good teammate?" During these types of exercises you will also likely learn something new.

During meetings, intentionally embrace and leverage the power of different views and approaches. While in the end, you ultimately can hold people accountable for their choices, this approach sends a very powerful message: "This is *your* team."

Also, take advantage of opportunities to cultivate Striver Attributes during interactions with outside entities. When meeting with or presenting to groups outside of your team—such as members of other teams, shareholders, stakeholders, the media, or the public—resist the temptation to go on and on about the great quarter your company just had. Focus on what went into what just happened by discussing what needs to be done individually and collectively to continue getting better. Inspire third parties by talking about how excited you are about the way your people are striving together.

Cultivate with Impact by Communicating Artfully

To cultivate with impact in all scenarios, *communicate artfully* by

- making good eye contact and projecting your voice,

- exercising the discipline to be concise,

- speaking slowly enough,

- increasing the "edge" in the tone of your voice for emphasis,

- occasionally raising or lowering your voice to gain (or regain) attention, and

- interjecting selectively, and occasionally imposing silence gaps to encourage others to speak up.

Be creative. Opportunities to cultivate Striver Attributes are limitless. Commit to building your company from the inside out. Over time the attributes will become embedded in your company's DNA, as a spirit of Strivership fills the air. Your people will be inspired to stretch themselves to unimaginable heights, and your quarterly earnings will exceed all expectations!

CHAPTER EIGHT

BUILDING CHAMPIONSHIP TEAMS IN SPORTS

The key is not the will to win. Everybody has that. It is the will to prepare to win that is important.

—Bob Knight

In sports, unlike the business world, talent plays a much larger role in who actually wins championships. Superior natural physical ability—qualities like speed, strength, and hand-eye coordination—provides a built-in advantage. This makes recruiting an important factor in every sport, but it's especially crucial in college tennis.

In my years at Texas, the majority of top recruits in the country went to Stanford. Eventually, Florida began making inroads with blue-chip recruits, including those who could not meet Stanford's tough admission standards.

The string of national titles that the Stanford program has won is astounding. Some coaches were dismissive of Stanford's success. "They always get the top players," was the common refrain. However, I had tremendous respect for the Stanford coach, Frank Brennan. If I'd been dismissive of his success I would not have been open to learning, and I learned a lot from him.

When I first came to Texas, I tried to emulate the Stanford model and failed miserably. I just did not have the ability or the desire to groom thoroughbreds. I was more excited about taming broncos. I was driven by the challenge of helping talented broncos learn to run straight.

Vickie Paynter definitely fit the bronco profile. She was an aggressive player who had been an exceptional all-around athlete in high school. When I recruited her, she had a strong national ranking, but not high enough to attract scholarship offers from the top schools. Few, if any, coaches thought she had the ability to become a top player in college. As one coach said to me, "She will help you in doubles and be solid at number five or six in singles." But Vickie had fire in her belly. She was itching to prove other coaches wrong about the kind of competitor she could become. I passed on two other recruits who were considered safer bets, and offered her a scholarship.

I was also able to sign Susan Gilchrist, who, despite being ranked higher than Vickie, had also not been recruited by a top school. Like Vickie, Susan was extremely aggressive, getting to the net whenever possible. She approached the game like a surgeon. Her lefty serve was precise and she could hit volleys with exquisite touch. She could hit drop volleys that landed on her opponent's side of the net with so much spin that the ball bounced back over to her side of the net! Susan's challenge was winning points when she wasn't on the attack. Her ground strokes needed work. Like Vickie, her game would have to evolve for her to compete consistently with players from top colleges.

Susan and Vickie combined with Carla Cossa, who had come to Texas a year earlier to inject new life into the program. I was excited about working with them in practice because they oozed self-motivation. When you are fortunate enough to coach athletes who want something for themselves more than you want it for them, they will stretch beyond their perceived limitations and special things can happen.

About two months before the start of Susan and Vickie's first year, I traveled to the National Hard Courts in Burlingame, California, to recruit for the next year's class. I was able to watch both of them compete in what would be one of their last junior events. Vickie advanced three or four rounds in the main draw, and then won a few more matches in the consolation draw. She had to wait a few days to return home because she had scheduled her nonrefundable flight to depart late on the last day of the tournament. On that day, as she waited in the clubhouse for a shuttle to take her to the airport, we were engaged in a conversation about the upcoming season when Stanford coach Frank Brennan approached us.

Frank and I exchanged pleasantries, and then he introduced himself to Vickie.

"I'm Frank Brennan. What's your name?"

"Vickie Paynter," she replied.

"Nice to meet you, Vickie. Where are you from?" he asked.

"Denville, New Jersey," she replied.

"Oh, I'm from New Jersey too," he said.

Vickie was offended he didn't know who she was. Afterward, she had a look on her face that screamed, "Someday, he'll know damn well who I am!" She had also attended camps conducted by coaches of other national powers and was told she wasn't good enough to play for a top school. Lots of players get turned down by top schools, but most respond to a perceived slight with something like, "Wait 'til we play them a year from now. I'll show that coach!" But instead of comparing, Vickie decided to compete. She hit the ground running by channeling this energy beginning on the first day of practice!

Vickie arrived at Texas in the fall and joined her new Longhorn teammates, all of whom had also been passed over by the top schools. They were determined to take down these schools, but they realized that they had a lot of ground to cover to catch them. As junior *players*, they had been good tennis players, but to accomplish seemingly unreachable goals, they would have to become better *competitors*. They understood this and proceeded to channel all of their energy into engaging fiercely, pushing each other to get better every day in practice.

> *Instead of hooking up the external motivation IV to channel animus toward schools that had rejected them, they embraced a spirit of Strivership, pouring their energies into striving together every day in practice.*

External motivation is like a drug. It makes you feel better in the short term, but keeps you from realizing any meaningful improvement. Instead of hooking up the external motivation IV to channel animus toward schools that had rejected them, they embraced a spirit of Strivership, pouring their energies into striving together every day in practice.

Three years later, the team pulled off a historic upset, beating Stanford in the semifinals of the NCAA Championships hosted by

Stanford. Vickie provided tremendous momentum for the historic victory by upsetting her Stanford opponent at number-two singles. After converting match point, instead of jumping up and down and making a scene, she looked over at her teammates and quietly but firmly pumped her fist. Vickie had competed every day in practice for three years. She had prepared for this.

In the finals, the team lost a close match to Florida, another perennial power. Being one of the last two teams left standing out of 283 at season's end had been a great accomplishment, but it wasn't enough for Vickie and her teammates. They wanted it all. But they knew that to win an NCAA Championship, they needed to get even better.

They wasted no time getting to work. During that summer, they traveled in small groups, pushing each other relentlessly while training together and playing as many professional tournaments as possible. They traveled without parents or private coaches. No entourage was necessary. It all came from within.

They carried this momentum into the next season, continuing to strive together every day in practice. I was a big believer in scheduling the toughest opponents possible, half at home and half on the road—preferably in hostile environments. Our regular season schedule was brutal and it showed. The team finished 26–5. This would be considered a successful season in most years. But no one predicts an NCAA Championship run in college tennis from a team entering the tournament with five losses.

But this wasn't your typical college tennis team. As assistant coach Lea Sauls used to say, "Of course they want to win, but even more than that, these players love the battle." Most teams need pep talks and lots of "You can do it!" exhortations going into matches. This group was usually too amped up before matches and needed to settle down. Assistant coach Vicki Ellis, who had been a team captain during her years as a Longhorn, did an extraordinary job of keeping them together and grounded. For my part, instead of giving pep talks, I did skits usually based on an off-the-wall silly theme. One time I brought a bag of dead crickets on the road collected from the halls of our tennis center during their annual spring infestation of the facility. I dumped the crickets on the floor during the prematch meeting and said, "I want you to feel like this is a home match!" The levity helped them to ratchet down their emotions, so they could focus on competing.

Seeded fifth, the team faced what seemed like insurmountable odds to win it all. They would have to defeat the ninth, third, first, and second seeds on consecutive days in the heat and humidity of Gainesville, Florida, in May. But no challenge could be too intimidating after all their fierce practices and the tough workouts that strength coach Angel Spassov had put them through in the weight room.

They attacked the challenge head on and charged through the draw, becoming the lowest-seeded team to win an NCAA Division I Tennis Championship. After defeating ninth-seeded USC, and avenging a regular season loss to number-three Duke, the team upset top-seeded Florida in the semis in front of two thousand screaming Gator fans. In the finals, the team pulled another upset against second-seeded Stanford. Paynter and Gilchrist clinched the victory at number-one doubles—a fitting end to their remarkable four-year journey.

I was extremely fortunate to be part of several special teams at Texas. Most of them did not win a national championship. Some reached the finals. Others only advanced as far as the Sweet Sixteen.

But almost all of them beat the odds. They weren't *winning teams,* they were *championship teams,* because they overachieved.

Winning teams are built from the outside in. These teams are full of Arrivers. The question, "How do we look to the outside world?" is what informs every decision. Arrivers will not reach beyond their grasp, because success must always be within their grasp. Any result that will enable them to compare favorably with the Competition will do.

Championship teams overachieve because they are built from the inside out. These teams are full of Strivers—athletes who constantly reach beyond their grasp. Athletes spend 80 percent of their time together practicing. Strivers are able to put thoughts about winning aside and focus on competing during practice—which I call 80 Percent Time.

Athletes with a champion's mind-set don't waste time thinking too much about what might happen when they face the Competition. They focus on *what goes into what could happen* by pushing themselves and each other during 80 Percent Time. Our championship teams exuded a spirit of Strivership, immersing themselves in the process of getting better every day.

Today it is extremely difficult for coaches to build championship teams. The term *sports entertainment business* once described professional sports. Now it describes sports organizations at all levels.

In youth sports and at the high school level, there is talk about cultivating the growth and development of young people. But it's just talk, meant to fit a marketing strategy that serves the interests of parents.

When a dad calls to say, "Johnnie's coach doesn't know what he's doing. He's being pushed too hard and he's not in the starting lineup enough," the appropriate response to the dad would be, "Please speak to the coach about this problem." But in too many cases, instead of standing up for the coach and by extension Johnnie, the administrator caves and intervenes on behalf of the parent.

Parents call the shots and they're making decisions based on what embellishes their child's resume. The ultimate goal? They want their child to "arrive" on a high school varsity roster and eventually on a college campus, scholarship in hand. I know many talented young coaches who have left the profession. They entered coaching expecting to be part of a transformative experience for young people, not to be part of a transactional relationship as a client services provider for parents. They signed up to develop Strivers, not Arrivers.

College coaches complain about recruiting pools full of Arrivers from the youth sports scene. You would think that colleges—institutions of higher learning—would recognize this problem and commit to developing Strivers. After all, colleges and universities are the last stop for young people before they enter an unstable, disruptive real world where they'll have to be Strivers to succeed.

Instead, colleges take the transactional approach to a whole new level. College presidents run their schools like corporate enterprises. A corporate approach works well in business where you're selling commodities or services, but not in schools where the "products" are people.

To counter the perception of corporatization, the NCAA has launched an aggressive PR campaign that ironically takes the focus off athletics. They run TV spots featuring athletes staring into the camera and exhorting, "Don't label me!" to remind us that they're not just athletes; they are *student*-athletes.

So the goal is to attend classes, study, and graduate? Okay. Phew! Glad we cleared that up! As one disappointed administrator told me, "The NCAA is promoting academics, well-being, and fairness as pillars of college athletics. Is that the bar we're setting? Those should be givens!"

College coaches are trapped in a catch-22. They are evaluated based on two criteria that are irreconcilable: "Where did your team finish?" and "Did your athletes have a 'positive' experience?" Coaches are expected to keep their athletes happy and produce winning teams.

These two goals are at cross-purposes. The vast majority of coaches cannot recruit a team of ready-made blue chips who will put their teams in the top twenty on talent alone. They must develop their athletes to be successful. And development requires stretching beyond perceived limitations. The problem is that stretching can be uncomfortable, which is okay until a parent or a donor calls to lodge a complaint.

Protecting athletes from discomfort stymies their ability to develop as athletes and as people. There is no growth without discomfort. Athletes on championship teams—teams that overachieve—embrace discomfort. Championship teams exude a competitive spirit—a spirit of Strivership—through a shared commitment to strive together every day. Winning cannot be controlled, but the willingness to strive together can be.

Protecting athletes from discomfort stymies their ability to develop as athletes and as people. There is no growth without discomfort.

This is what Alabama football coach Nick Saban calls "The Process." Saban's former associate head coach Burton Burns described him as "a competitor" rather than "a winner." He said, "If you compete, the other thing will happen." In other words, if you compete, you put yourself in the best possible position to win. You put yourself in position to achieve beyond expectations![16]

I help coaches in a wide variety of sports build championship teams. Lots of coaches talk about "The Process." Great coaches have learned how to create an environment that inspires their athletes to focus on "The Process." Their teams exude a spirit—a sense that everyone involved is excited about getting better every day.

To imbue a spirit of Strivership in your program, you must

- articulate a purpose-driven vision,

- foster trusting relationships,

- cultivate Striver Attributes by setting stretch goals,

- cultivate Striver Attributes by modeling Strivership,

- cultivate Striver Attributes by designing uncomfortable practices,

- cultivate Striver Attributes by intentionally planting the seeds of Strivership, and

- cultivate with impact by communicating artfully.

Articulate a Vision That Speaks to a Higher Purpose

Your vision should inspire your people to stretch beyond their limitations to achieve beyond expectations. One coach I have worked with has expressed her program's vision this way: "Our program will consistently put the most competitive team in the country on the field."

---

16 Marc Tracy, "Why Nick Saban Is the Ultimate Masochist," *New York Times*, January 9, 2018, https://www.nytimes.com/2018/01/09/sports/alabama-nick-saban.html.

Foster Trusting Relationships

Do this by demonstrating a genuine concern for your athletes as people first and athletes second. Build these relationships by making a commitment to learn about each athlete. Put your views on the shelf and immerse yourself in their world by asking questions. Make this effort during informal moments as well as during scheduled get-togethers. Efforts to foster trusting relationships should be ongoing and never-ending.

Set Stretch Goals

You may have certain goals in mind, but keep asking questions until your athletes come up with goals that require them to stretch beyond their perceived limitations. In the end, a goal must be viewed as their idea. By taking them through this process you will be cultivating Striver Attributes in your athletes.

Model Strivership

Sports programs are a reflection of their head coach. The most powerful way to cultivate Striver Attributes is to *model* them. This is not easy to do. When everything around you is chaotic you must remain calm and clear thinking, even if it's an act. The nonverbal cues that you give off in the process will have a huge impact on your athletes. The impact of modeling is often underestimated because it is not always immediately discernable.

Modeling takes discipline. It is one of the most difficult things to learn during the transition from athlete to coach. One minute you're wearing your emotions on your sleeve and the next moment you're having to at least appear comfortable with being uncomfortable. Coaches who manage are scoreboard watchers. Coaches who lead exude a love for the battle by modeling Striver Attributes in all relationships.

In Relationship to Self, leaders model the willingness to

- move outside their comfort zone,

- solve difficult problems unconventionally,

- learn new skills,

- persevere through adversity, and

- present an accurate self-image.

In Relationship to Team, leaders model the willingness to

- be assertive and challenge teammates,

- support teammates,

- demonstrate empathy for teammates, and

- communicate directly in a timely manner with the source when issues arise with a teammate.

In Relationship to Boss, leaders model the willingness to

- be assertive by offering their boss new ideas,

- support their boss, and

- communicate directly in a timely manner with their boss when issues arise.

Design Uncomfortable Practices

You cannot possibly cultivate these Striver Attributes in your athletes unless you put them in situations in practice that challenge them to demonstrate the attributes. Athletes spend 80 percent of their time together in practice preparing to face the Competition. To fully prepare them to face the Competition you must design uncomfortable practices. Design your practices while assuming that every team on your schedule will be a nightmare to face. Prepare your athletes for this by putting them in situations where they must problem-solve by executing at a high level under pressure. The definition of competing in sports is *making the opposition uncomfortable with purpose-driven execution.*

When athletes compete, three dynamics are being stressed simultaneously at all times:

- emotional dynamic—control of impulses and empathy

- mental dynamic—problem solving

- physical dynamic—skills and fitness

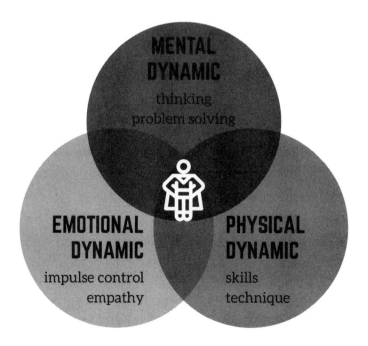

Athletes must develop a Competitive Mind-Set during 80 percent of their time rather than a Practice Mind-Set. Developing a Competitive Mind-Set requires creating a positive transfer of learning from practice to competition.

A Practice Mind-Set creates a transfer of learning from practice to practice because practice is designed based on the physical dynamic. The focus is on technique. Athletes submit to a heavy volume of mind-numbing blocked and serial drills to isolate specific skills. They are not challenged to problem-solve, so the mental dynamic is not stressed, and the only emotional challenge they face is enduring the tedium of being on autopilot. And when you face the Competition you cannot afford to go on autopilot!

A Competitive Mind-Set creates a positive transfer of learning from practice to competition because the design of practice is based on the mental dynamic. When facing the Competition, athletes are constantly compelled to process and respond to three variables:

- Where am I?

- What's coming at me?

- Where is the opposition?

The pressure to constantly process and respond to these variables forces athletes to move out of their comfort zone. They are challenged to use their skills to problem-solve. And they are challenged emotionally, not by tedium, but by the pressure to constantly adapt and make adjustments.

Practices are not truly competitive if you simply reinforce winning. A practice philosophy based purely on a desire to win does not optimally prepare a team to shine when winning really counts. Of course, athletes want to win in practice, but unless they are focused on *making the opposition uncomfortable with purpose-driven execution*, they will not be prepared to win when it's time to face the Competition.

To develop a Competitive Mind-Set, challenge your athletes to make each other *uncomfortable with purpose-driven execution* by designing practices based on problem solving using these scenarios:

- *Drills*—Blocked and serial drills that mimic set tactical patterns. Use drills to lead into game situations.

- *Game Situations*—Games that involve complex tactical execution with restrictions and parameters applied to provide context, compelling your athletes to problem-solve and *make the opposition uncomfortable with purpose-driven execution.*

- *Scrimmaging*—Live competition designed to work on sustaining the ability to *make the opposition uncomfortable with purpose-driven execution.*

To trigger problem solving in drills and game situations:

- Sequence to build from simple to complex.

- Emphasize that the goal of scoring is "learning how to compete," not "winning the drill."

- Occasionally let things get messy, allowing your athletes to become uncomfortable.

- Conclude before the learning curve flattens. Err on the side of ending prematurely.

- Avoid creating scenarios that require athletes to cater to each other. Keep it real.

To organize practices in a way that facilitates the development of a Competitive Mind-Set:

- Arrive at practice thoroughly prepared.

- Make certain that the practice area is set up in advance.

- Make it clear that in most cases, only you, the head coach, can stop practice.

- Assign assistant coaches roles that support your role as conductor of practice.

- Keep people moving between drills by keeping banter to a minimum.

- Schedule water breaks every twenty minutes.

- Ensure that interaction with coaches during breaks does not drag on.

- Make certain that the practice space is clear and safe going into each drill.

Intentionally Plant the Seeds of Strivership

When your athletes are compelled to make each other *uncomfortable with purpose-driven execution* they will be challenged to exhibit Striver Attributes. This creates openings for you to intentionally plant the seeds of Strivership by cultivating these attributes. In every situation, instead of focusing on *what just happened,* zero in on what *went into what just happened.* Engage your athletes with questions and observations when they demonstrate or fail to demonstrate the attributes instead of simply relying on talking/instructing/directing/correcting.

For example, let's say that during your basketball practice the second string defeated your heavily favored first string. One of the second stringers played a huge under-the-radar role in the victory by moving well outside of his comfort zone to hold the team's leading scorer well under his average. Do you acknowledge this fact? Of course. But then quickly pivot to observations like: "You were on an island today! You really had to put yourself out there to get this done!" or questions like: "How were you able to read almost every type of screen they used to keep him from gaining separation? I can count on one hand the number of quality looks he got today!"

Evaluate your athletes during both practices and games based on their willingness to compete—their willingness *to stress opponents with purpose-driven execution,* and to respond proactively when opponents stress them in return! Cultivating Striver Attributes is a way of evaluating that has the most meaningful and lasting effect.

Seize opportunities to plant the seeds of Strivership by cultivating Striver Attributes with incisive questions and observations like the following examples:

Relationship to Self:
- "You really had to put yourself out there to get this done!" (moving out of comfort zone)

- "Accept this challenge. Jump into the fire. You can do this!" (moving out of comfort zone)

- "This needs to be better! How are you going to make it better? Figure it out. You can do it!" (problem solving)

- "Wow! How the heck did you figure that out? What did you see that I missed?" (problem solving)

- "Sally, can you get this corner kick organized?" (problem solving)

- "What are your pressure release options in that situation?" (problem solving)

- "What obstacles stand in your way? How are you going to overcome them?" (problem solving)

- "Have you approached this problem from every possible angle?" (problem solving)

- "How did you attack that problem?" (problem solving)

- "You never stop learning!" (learning new things)

- "Are you willing to learn this new technique to raise your level?" (learning new things)

- "You had to overcome so many obstacles to get to this point!" (embracing failure)

- "Push through this. You can do it." (embracing failure)

- "What do you really think?!" (authenticity)

- "One thing I respect about you is that what I see is what I get!" (authenticity)

Relationship to Team:

- "Are you prepared to compete in practice today, or just play?" (challenging teammates)

- "Are you ready to suffer in practice, so you can make your opponents suffer in November?" (challenging teammates)

- "What are you going to work on in practice today to keep your man from getting a quality look at the basket?" (challenging teammates)

- "How can you challenge your teammates to get better?" (challenging teammates)

- "I appreciate your willingness to challenge each other. Remember, what happens at practice stays at practice. Let's go eat." (challenging and supporting teammates)

- "Sam (the quiet one), what do you think?" (challenging teammates and demonstrating empathy)

- "Katie (not particularly well-liked at the time), you were a catalyst in practice today!" (challenging teammates and demonstrating empathy)

- "Jim, if you have an issue with Bill, address it directly with him." (communicating with teammates)

- "When you leave practice, talk to each other. Remember ... triangulation is a disease!" (communicating with teammates)

Relationship to Coach:
- "I need pushback." (challenging the coach)

- "I am getting tired of being the motivator! Who's going to step up?" (challenging the coach)

- "What do we need to be doing differently?" (challenging the coach)

- "How do you think practice went? What are your thoughts?" (communicating with the coach)

- "Do not hesitate to bring problems to me. You will be heard!" (communicating with the coach)

- "Thank you for coming in today. Now we're on the same page." (communicating with the coach)

Take advantage of opportunities to plant the seeds of Strivership outside of practice as well. Seize opportunities to cultivate Striver Attributes in these scenarios:

- individual meetings

- team meetings

- casual bump-ins

- interactions with outside entities

- your team's postseason self-evaluation

During individual meetings with your athletes to discuss individual goals, focus on planting the seeds of Strivership instead of zeroing in on outcomes. Remember, you want them to stretch, not settle. Challenge your athletes to continue to stretch themselves beyond their perceived limitations by evaluating them based on their willingness to compete—to strive together—with questions like:

- "How do you plan to contribute to the pursuit of the team goal?"

- "What can you do to get better? Are you willing to step out of your comfort zone to learn that skill?"

- "How can you help your teammates get better? Are the lines of direct communication open?"

- "How can your teammates help you get better? How can you be pushed to execute better under pressure?"

- "How can I help you get better?"

Of course, you will want to let your athletes know where they stand with regard to results. But cultivating Striver Attributes usually yields far better results!

During these meetings pay close attention to the strength of each athlete's willingness to be *self-accountable* for contributing to the shared commitment to achieving team goals. As Abraham Lincoln once said, "Always bear in mind that your own resolution to succeed is more important than any other."

You can also use team meetings to cultivate Striver Attributes in your athletes by focusing on guided questions as opposed to simply telling them what to do. If there is a problem to solve or an issue to address, instead of weighing in heavily right away ask your athletes questions to move them toward a resolution. This approach to a team meeting cultivates the willingness to move out of one's comfort zone, problem-solve unconventionally, and challenge teammates—as well as a willingness to challenge you.

Another way to use team meetings to cultivate Striver Attributes is to facilitate sessions where your athletes determine *the essential attributes of a Striver*. Again, you would ask questions to get them to a certain place. You could also facilitate a session where your athletes determine what should be *the expectations of a good teammate*.

Along the way you will very likely learn something new as well!

In all of these sessions, intentionally embrace and leverage the power of different views and approaches. While you ultimately can hold them accountable for their choices, this approach sends a very powerful message: "This is *your* team."

Casual bump-ins can also be used to cultivate Striver Attributes. These interactions are similar in concept to walk-arounds, except that they are serendipitous for both parties. Legendary University of

Texas football coach Darrell Royal talked about how he was always coaching, even during casual bump-ins with players on campus.

Also, take advantage of opportunities to cultivate Striver Attributes in your athletes indirectly through third parties. When meeting with or presenting to groups outside of your team—such as members of other teams, administrators, stakeholders, the media, and the public—resist the temptation to go on and on about results and focus on areas of improvement as well as what needs to be done individually and collectively to continue getting better.

Communicate Artfully

To cultivate with impact in all of these scenarios, communicate artfully by

- making good eye contact and projecting your voice,

- exercising the discipline to be concise,

- speaking slowly enough,

- increasing the "edge" in the tone of your voice for emphasis,

- occasionally raising or lowering your voice to gain (or regain) attention, and

- imposing gaps of silence when you feel that it's time for your athletes to speak up.

Remember Kelly Pace and Lucie Ludvigova from chapter 3? When they were seniors, it was very clear that they were the leaders of the team. They had no choice! The rest of the starting lineup that season included a sophomore and at least two first-year students. They were a talented crew, but they had not been through the kinds of trials and tribulations that Lucie and Kelly had during their college careers.

The two seniors were ready to lead, but if the team was going to do something special they would have to cultivate emerging leaders.

One of those emerging leaders was Cristina Moros. Cristina was the first blue-chip recruit that I had signed since my early years at Texas. It had been a long time since I'd recruited someone to whom the top schools had offered a scholarship. Cristina was a highly ranked singles player and number-one in the world in junior doubles. She walked onto campus with a bit of a swagger, as if to say, "I know my new teammates have had some success in college, but I just played at the US Open!"

It's not that her attitude was off-putting; that wasn't Cristina's nature. Like most highly decorated young athletes, she was conveying a classic Arriver mentality. She had *arrived* at Texas on a wave of junior glory and to some degree she assumed success would ensue.

As a younger coach, I fought this attitude. I had come from a team sports background where teammates who took themselves too seriously were quickly put in their place. I had to learn the value of empathy the hard way. Tennis is an individual sport. If I had been in Cristina's shoes, I'm sure that I would have given off a similar aura. Instead of giving her a stern talking-to, I asked Lucie if she'd like to take Cristina on the court for a workout. We were still a couple of weeks away from the start of official practice. The NCAA, in all its wisdom, restricts the amount of time coaches can work with their athletes. Anything the players did at this point had to be on their own.

Lucie and Cristina arranged to hit on a very hot August afternoon. I had not done my daily cardio workout yet that day, so I wheeled an exercise bike from our training room to an obscured location, two courts away from where they were playing. After warming up, Lucie asked Cristina if she wanted to play minitennis, a game played in a small area of the court bordered by the service line and the singles sidelines. Cristina agreed, and then Lucie explained that at Texas, we play minitennis with two special rules: you cannot hit the ball hard and you cannot come to the net. These rules made the game come down to who could exhibit the best combination of movement, placement, touch, and want-to! Cristina was an excellent athlete with tremendous hands. I'm sure in her mind, a Czech player she'd never heard of before could not possibly match her skills.

Lucie not only matched Cristina's skills; with pinpoint placement and touch she made Cristina visit every part of her side of the court. When Cristina was able to pressure her, Lucie did not miss. Making an error of any kind was a cardinal sin to Lucie. Every ball came back! She was intent on making Cristina *uncomfortable with purpose-driven execution.* They played to 11 and Lucie won 11–2. As Cristina bent over, panting and exhausted, Lucie walked up the net and said, "Eyes on me!" Then she told her, "We do this every day *before* practice. Do you want to play another one?"

Without hesitation Cristina replied, "No, I'm good."

Cristina went on that season to play a crucial role in a miracle comeback the team staged to win a second NCAA Championship for the program. The key to winning that championship was the leadership that Lucie and Kelly had demonstrated during the off-season. During each practice, they would model what it meant to compete, starting with gnarly minitennis matches that created tension that you could cut with a knife. They also took all of the young players to some off-campus courts on NCAA-mandated days off (from coaches) and put them through tough practices. I did not know about these workouts because the seniors did not tell me. They had no desire to score points with me. Impression management had not come into vogue yet. After these workouts, Kelly and Lucie would take their young teammates out to eat and hang out. Any tension that had brewed during the practice was left on the court. Kelly and Lucie understood that great teams live a Jekyll and Hyde existence, engaging fiercely in the arena and supporting each other unconditionally outside of it.

The next year we faced Duke in the quarterfinals of the NCAA Championships, hosted by Florida State in brutal conditions. The match came down to number-one doubles. Cristina and Farley Taylor were our top team, and they were one of the best doubles teams in the country. Under normal circumstances, we would have had good reason to be optimistic. But near the end of her singles match, Cristina had started to cramp. The combination of unusually high heat and humidity had taken its toll on several players throughout the tournament. Cristina was our leader, and I could tell that in her own quiet way she was carrying the weight of the team on her back. By the time her singles finished, she was in extreme pain and could barely move. Our trainer, Tina Bonci, advised against letting her continue, but Cristina insisted on playing doubles. Tina taped her right leg tightly from hip to toe, and Cristina limped onto the court ready to compete.

I tried to place Cristina in positions where she would not be required to cover much ground. Meanwhile, Farley would have to cover much more ground than usual, and that's exactly what she did. She did so playing a much more disruptive role at the net when Cristina was serving, or by returning and running down lobs that Cristina normally would have put away with her overhead. Amazingly, they were able to extend the match to a third-set tie-breaker. On match point for the Duke team, Cristina dove for a volley that she was not able to reach and collapsed on the court. She had to be carried off the court on a stretcher to the training room where she was given fluids intravenously.

The courage Cristina demonstrated on that day was inspiring, but she was well prepared for it. Cristina will tell you that the two seniors on her first team, Lucie Ludvigova and Kelly Pace, taught her how to compete. The leadership torch had been passed from Gilchrist and Paynter to Pace and Ludvigova, who passed it along to Moros.

What role did I play in all of this? I must have put them through a rigorous leadership training program with a reading list featuring best-selling leadership experts, right? This is the conventional twenty-first-century approach to developing leaders. Unfortunately, it's why we have fewer leaders than ever before.

I didn't teach them how to lead. Leadership cannot be taught. I sought to cultivate leadership in my athletes by conveying my belief that they could stretch *beyond* their perceived limitations to achieve *beyond* expectations. Tennis great Rafael Nadal once said: "I learned to enjoy suffering during my career." Athletes develop leadership abilities when they are challenged to demonstrate Striver Attributes in response to the suffering they encounter during 80 Percent Time.

Your administrators can help you plant the seeds of Strivership by structuring their postseason evaluations to cultivate Striver Attributes in your athletes. At the same time these administrators would be impressing upon your athletes what the department stands for with two very powerful messages to athletes:

1. "We are holding *you* accountable to demonstrating these attributes."

2. "We are empowering *your coaches* to cultivate these attributes."

3. Consider sending out an evaluation survey like this one that has been used by several of my clients.

Results from this survey will help us continue to improve all aspects of our athletic department as we strive for competitive excellence.

For each statement, please write the number that applies.

1 = Always   2 = Most of the Time   3 = Occasionally
4 = Seldom   5 = Never

During this past season:

_____ I accepted responsibility for my own actions.

_____ The head coach expected all team members to be in excellent physical condition at the start of official practices.

_____ The head coach challenged me to stretch myself to compete at an increasingly higher level.

_____ I accepted constructive criticism from the coaches.

_____ I demonstrated persistence when confronted with adversity in practice.

_____ I challenged teammates in practice with purpose-driven execution.

_____ I supported all of my teammates.

_____ I communicated directly with a teammate when a serious issue arose.

_____ I demonstrated support for the head coach.

_____ I communicated directly with the head coach if a serious issue arose.

_____ The head coach made me feel heard when I approached her/him with an issue.

Name: _____

Sport: _____

By beginning each statement with "I," you are calling on athletes to be self-accountable—a quality sorely lacking in today's young people, who have been conditioned to look to others to keep them accountable.

Unfortunately, most administrators send out a very different kind of survey to athletes with questions related to the coach's knowledge of tactics, ability to run an effective practice, and organizational skills. And, in most cases, the athletes are not even required to sign the surveys. It's important to let athletes know that the lines of communication are open, but feedback from them should be communicated directly to the coach face-to-face in individual or team meetings.

Asking young athletes to evaluate the performance of experienced professionals is ridiculous. The life experience of most eighteen- to twenty-one-year-old athletes consists of attending school and playing sports. Asking more open-ended question like "How could your experience have been better?" is fine, but allowing them to rate the coach's abilities is simply extending an open invitation for them to complain about and weigh in on things they know nothing about.

More importantly, the process serves to undermine the coach's efforts to cultivate Striver Attributes and, by extension, self-accountability.

If no one truly holds athletes accountable, how are they going to develop the strong sense of self needed to excel in their sport? And a strong sense of self becomes even more important after graduation, when they must quickly transition from the linear, predictable world of college to the real world. There are no anxiety-free zones in the disruptive, unstable twenty-first-century economy.

Coaches have a unique and special opportunity to make a difference in young people's lives. My son Tim, who has extensive experience in both school administration and coaching, has noted that coaches often know students even better than the teachers do. "The student comments submitted by coaches are often much more insightful because they're in a competitive cauldron together," he says. The best coaches base their relationship with their athletes on "respect," not "like." Over time, the like level increases. A relationship based on respect forges a much deeper bond.

The depth of this bond does not typically surface during the obligatory athlete exit interview at the end of four years. But if you ask an athlete who has been out of school five to ten years, "How did your coach make a difference in your life?" you're likely to get a very meaningful response.

I witnessed this firsthand as a parent. My son Andy played basketball at Lafayette College for longtime, highly successful coach Fran O'Hanlon. At the beginning of his career at Lafayette, Andy did not like Coach O'Hanlon. Coach O. had started the opening meeting Andy's first year by saying, "I'm not here to pat you on the back." Andy had been a star in high school, so he was accustomed to receiving regular pats on the back. Coach O. put tremendous pressure on Andy and his teammates to execute at a high level under pressure. Praise was rare. It had to be earned.

When Andy expressed dislike for him, it was music to my ears, because I knew what Coach O. was up to. He was cultivating Striver Attributes in Andy by pushing him out of his comfort zone and putting him in situations where he had to solve difficult problems. I knew that deep down Andy respected Coach O. Over time a mutual respect evolved. Now, eight years after graduating, Andy has his own team. He works for a social media marketing company as a project manager and quotes Coach O. regularly to coworkers. The tech industry is extraordinarily competitive, but Andy is prepared. As he told me recently, "No one could ever put more pressure on me than Coach O. did."

I have worked with dozens of high school and college coaches who are ready to be unleashed. Most of them are effectively running in place, trying to balance the two conflicting expectations: "keep 'em happy" and "win." Many have simply resigned themselves to struggling with this ridiculous balancing act by playing politics in an effort to keep their jobs.

Although most young athletes have been conditioned to be Arrivers, many are tired of being coddled and told they're special. When you challenge them to take their performance to another level, their eyes light up. No one has ever asked them to do more! When they are asked to stretch, they think, "Wow! My coach thinks I can get even better."

There are very few leaders in athletics today. *Leaders* are willing to challenge convention. It's time for colleges and high schools to follow the lead of championship companies like Southwest Airlines and start building their programs from the inside out. Instead of channeling Bobby McFerrin by chanting, "Don't worry. Be happy," how about "Let's get excited about competing—about striving together!" The first athletics leader who decides to genuinely empower coaches by imbuing a spirit of Strivership will not only win more; he or she will fuel the growth and development of tomorrow's Strivers.

CHAPTER NINE

IMBUING A SPIRIT OF STRIVERSHIP IN SCHOOLS

Were all instructors to realize that the quality of mental process, not the production of correct answers, is the measure of educative growth, something hardly less than a revolution in teaching would be worked.

—John Dewey, *Democracy and Education*, 1916

It's 2019 and we're still waiting for the revolution! In the 103 years since Dewey put forth his vision, there has been no systemic disruption of the learning model in our education system. The system is still designed to produce Arrivers, young people conditioned to play the game of school. Students are graded based on how much information they can retain on a test—disconnected, disassociated information that they forget within a few months.

At the same time, in an Age of Innovation, companies are searching for Strivers: people who can invent, adapt, and reinvent their jobs. Young people must quickly transition from school, where they simply come up with the answers the teacher is looking for, to the real world, where they will be challenged to tackle problems that do not yet have answers.

> *Young people must quickly transition from school, where they simply come up with the answers the teacher is looking for, to the real world, where they will be challenged to tackle problems that do not yet have answers.*

I'm sure that some of the people who run our schools would like to make the bold changes required to develop Strivers. But they're up against a powerful "test 'em, grade 'em, and rank 'em" lobby controlled by politicians and strongly influenced by parents. Schools have become corporatized diploma mills. Reducing students to numbers fits the needs of both groups. Politicians rely on measurables to sway voters and parents use them to build their children's resumes.

There are many teachers working at these schools who would love to be freed from this transactional stranglehold. Twelve years ago, I met one of those teachers.

One day early in my first year as athletics director at Trinity Episcopal, I was in the gym having a discussion with one of our basketball coaches when all of a sudden I heard a student at the far end of the building yell, "Mr. Moore! Mr. Moore!"

I thought to myself, "Wow, a student is seeking me out. This is unusual, but it's kind of nice!" As an AD, my "team" was now the coaches. I missed close connections with students. My hopes were dashed, however, when I turned around and saw the student chasing after Trinity's other Mr. Moore—math teacher Kevin Moore. I would soon discover that in many ways Kevin's approach to teaching mirrored my approach to coaching.

Kevin Moore is a rail-thin six-foot-four African American with a long stride, a quick smile, and a deep James Earl Jones–like voice. At different times during his years at Trinity Episcopal, he taught math and social studies at both the elementary and middle school levels. Kevin was a pied piper to his students, but not in the same way as many teachers who achieve that status. He was not out to win favor with his students by becoming their buddy. And he could not relate to them as an athlete. He used to joke that everyone assumed he'd played basketball because he was tall and African American. In truth, he had little interest in sports.

Kevin was one of the most popular teachers at Trinity. When the prestigious Harlem Success Academies tried to recruit him, administrators and parents bent over backward trying to keep him from leaving. When he decided to stay, it was announced to the entire school at chapel and he received a standing ovation. Kevin could do no wrong in the eyes of administrators because the parents loved him. And in today's customer-friendly independent school environment, parents drive everything. They are paying outrageous sums of money to send their children to these schools. In effect the parents, not the students, are the customers.

Most of the parents loved Kevin Moore for one simple reason: their kids loved him. But most parents had no idea *why* their kids loved him. Initially, it was a puzzle to me as well. How did this humble, highly intellectual young man who spoke like a college professor make this magical connection with students of all ages?

During the week he taught classes at Trinity, but during weekends I'd run into him at a coffee shop tutoring high school seniors in calculus. And quite often former Trinity students who had become young adults would come back to campus to see him.

One day, I decided to visit one of his classes in an attempt to discover the secret to his powers of connectivity. The minute I entered his classroom I was struck by how engaged his students were with him, but even more so how engaged they were with each other. Kevin was not standing in front of his students while they sat in neat rows dutifully following his instructions. They were divided into teams scattered around the room. This was a social studies class working on an issue relating to American history. Kevin provided each team with a specific question about the issue. They were then asked to break out with their teams to discuss the question at hand. Before each team got to work, they were asked to select a scribe who would take notes and a presenter who would present the team's findings to the rest of the class.

Kevin sent them off and then walked around the room, stopping to listen in on each team's discussion and posing questions when he deemed it necessary to facilitate the flow. When he sensed that all of the teams were ready to put forth their position he brought everyone back together and asked the presenter for each team to come forward and report to the class. Kevin urged classmates to politely interrupt presenters when they felt the need to ask for clarification or elaboration. He also interrupted them occasionally to ask his own challenging questions. He also did not want students to hesitate challenging him. In fact, he heavily encouraged pushback.

I was stunned. This was Strivership in the classroom! Most of the parents did not realize that, although students did like Mr. Moore, the foundation of his enormous popularity was a deeply held respect they had for him. Most of the adults in their lives were urging them to keep success within clutching distance so that they could meet expectations. Kevin was challenging them to reach beyond their grasp to achieve *beyond* expectations.

Kevin is not a *teacher*. He is a *cultivator* of learning. His approach to teaching aligns with constructivism. A constructivist provides a framework for students from which they can construct their own learning. When schools choose to be identified with approaches like Montessori, design thinking, and project-based learning, they are adopting a pedagogy. They are following a preconceived methodology. Constructivism is a philosophy, not a pedagogy. And it's a philosophy that has been around since Plato's time.

A couple of years after I left Trinity Episcopal to start my consulting business, Kevin took a similar path. He realized that working in almost any traditional school was limiting his professional growth. Conventional schooling is structured to be a station-to-station experience. There is a lot of talk about critical thinking and innovation, but the overarching goal of the core curriculum in mainstream schools is to deliver information to students who are then tested on their retention of that information in hopes of advancing to the next grade.

Kevin joined a couple of his colleagues from Trinity, Lisa Zapalac and Cathy Lewis, to build two enterprises. They established The Number Lab, a consulting business that brings teachers to Austin and trains them how to use the principles of constructivism in their classrooms. They also started a microschool called Long-View, where they directly apply the principles of constructivism.

At Long-View, teachers prepare students for life success, not school success, by challenging them to solve difficult problems. They are evaluated based on their ability to tackle those problems.

Long-View does not reduce students to numbers by issuing grades based on how much disconnected, disassociated information they can retain. The bar is set much higher. Teachers write narratives based on observation and on interviews that they conduct with each student. They focus on criteria that challenge students to move out of their comfort zones and strive together.

In *Relationship to Self*, Long-View teachers cultivate in their students the willingness to *solve problems unconventionally* while *learning new skills* and *embracing failure.* They cultivate these Striver Attributes by challenging them to

- take initiative,

- question deeply,

- generate original ideas,

- experiment with newer, still "fragile" concepts, and

- transform insights into new concepts.

In *Relationship to Team*, Long-View teachers cultivate in their students the willingness to *challenge classmates* while demonstrating *support* and exhibiting *empathy* for them, and *communicating* directly with classmates when issues arise. They cultivate these Striver Attributes, challenging them to

- give and accept feedback,

- persuade,

- negotiate,

- back up their positions with logic,

- actively listen, and

- work with a group to solve a challenge that would be difficult to tackle alone.

In *Relationship to Teacher*, students at Long-View do not offer unconditional respect for their teachers. And unlike at most mainstream schools, the teachers are not looking for it. Long-View teachers cultivate in their students a willingness to *challenge them with new ideas,* and strongly encourage them to *communicate* directly with them if they are confused or upset with something that a teacher has said or done.

Long-View prepares students for the realities of the world that they will enter as young adults. The school was named to make the point that parents should be taking the "long view" when thinking about their children's future. The criteria they use to evaluate students mirror expectations they will face when they become young adults.

Unfortunately, mainstream schools are not developing tomorrow's Strivers. Administrators typically come up through the ranks solidly entrenched in traditional pedagogy. The addition of extracurriculars like "think tanks" and "design labs" has helped, but the primary emphasis in schools remains unchanged: grinding for grades. The focus is on scoring high on tests covering disassociated, detached information, most of which students will soon forget.

The education business model has changed with the advent of technologies like online classes, but the "learning" model remains the same. Innovations like distance learning simply provide a different (lucrative) way to promote the test 'em, grade 'em, and rank 'em approach that's been in place since the nineteenth century!

I have a vivid memory of a meeting I had with my tenth-grade advisor to review my performance over the previous semester. He summed up the review by saying, "Jeff, the one observation that all of your teachers agreed on is that when you are interested in a subject you do really well. If you commit to doing your best in all of your classes your GPA will rise significantly." I remember thinking to myself, "Why would I want to work hard on something I'm not interested in? And where is 'doing my best' at taking tests going to get me?"

I viewed school as a means to an end, not "the end." I wanted to get the credential so I could get out in the world and actually start doing something! Getting straight As requires conformity. Having an influential career demands originality.

In a *New York Times* article "Are Straight A's Always a Good Thing?" Adam Grant, a professor at University of Pennsylvania's Wharton School of Business, remembers one particularly alarming experience with a student who stopped by his office. "He sat down and burst into tears. My mind started cycling through a list of events that could make a college junior cry: His girlfriend had dumped him; he had been accused of plagiarism. 'I just got my first A-minus,' he said, his voice shaking. Year after year, I watch in dismay as students obsess over getting straight As. Some sacrifice their health; a few have even tried to sue their school after falling short. All have joined the cult of perfectionism out of a conviction that top marks are a ticket to elite graduate schools and lucrative job offers."[17]

This "cult of perfectionism" has contributed to ever-increasing stress levels experienced by students in our schools. During the past decade, anxiety has overtaken depression as the most common reason college students seek counseling services. In a study of college students, the American College Health Association found that 62

---

17 Jeremy Engle, "Are Straight A's Always a Good Thing?" *New York Times*, December 11, 2018, https://www.nytimes.com/2018/12/11/learning/are-straight-as-always-a-good-thing.html.

percent of those surveyed reported that they had experienced "over-whelming anxiety" the previous year.[18]

In my view, schools have been exacerbating this problem by *protecting* students from anxiety. They are intentionally conditioning young people to *avoid* anxiety at all costs—even the kind of anxiety that can help them grow and develop.

Challenging Tradition

A group of K–12 independent school leaders has come together to confront this issue head on. Led by Scott Looney, the head of the Hawken School in suburban Cleveland, they have formed the Mastery Transcript Consortium. These leaders are positioned to trigger the first systemic disruption of the American learning model in the history of the education industry by ending the archaic test 'em, grade 'em, and rank 'em model of assessing students. The MTC model of assessment is organized around mastery standards, not grades.

The following admonitions on the consortium website indicate that members clearly recognize the negative impact that the "cult of perfectionism" in schools is having on young people.

> *We hear it all the time, particularly from students themselves.*
> *School hurts. Too many students leave high school uninspired,*
> *under-prepared, and anxious about the world that awaits*
> *them. Why? Our schools are tasked primarily with sorting*
> *and ranking them, rather than engaging and enlightening*

---

18   Benoit Denizet-Lewis, "Why Are More American Teenagers Than Ever Suffering From Severe Anxiety?" *New York Times*, October 11, 2017, https://www.nytimes.com/2017/10/11/magazine/why-are-more-american-teenagers-than-ever-suffering-from-severe-anxiety.html.

them. A complex human being is reduced to simple numbers and letters. We can do better.[19]

The test 'em, grade 'em, and rank 'em system has been essentially outdated since John Dewey called for a revolution in 1916. But during the Industrial Age, there was no strong movement to disrupt the system because product cycles were much longer, so change was incremental. Thus, problem solving was a more straightforward process.

Had you asked CEOs during the Industrial Age about how they were going to overcome their biggest challenges, they would have probably answered with a standard go-to, such as "better management discipline." But in the twenty-first-century economy, their overwhelming response is "coping with rapid and constant change." Product cycles have shortened dramatically. Many, if not most, problems either have more than one possible solution or no solution at all. And knowledge deficiencies (i.e., what you know) can be remedied quickly online. The key to success is no longer what you know, but what you can do with what you know.

That raises the question: Are our schools effectively preparing children for this new real world? The answer is, in most cases, no. What is the goal of academics? Is it to prepare children for the real world, or is it to provide them with lots of knowledge about disconnected subjects for memorization? If our goal is the latter, we're doing an outstanding job. If we want to prepare children to succeed in the real world, we will have to concede that our current educational system is failing to do so.

If we return to Google's research, we see that the company found no correlation between someone's ability to perform at school and his

---

19 Mastery Transcript Consortium, https://mastery.org.

or her performance on the job at Google. That's because grades do not assess the ability to apply knowledge and use creativity to solve problems.

To prepare young people for the real world, schools should be focused on developing Strivers, not grade grinders. Teachers must cultivate Striver Attributes in their students, challenging them to move out of their comfort zones by putting them in problem-solving scenarios. The scenarios should include problems that require creative problem solving. Outside of extracurricular programs, mainstream schools still focus on using established methods to solve problems. Companies are being compelled to continually adapt and change course, while schools continue to lead students down a well-marked path.

Hopefully, bold new initiatives by schools like Long-View and groups like MTC will influence school leaders to take action, not just in elementary and secondary schools, but also at the college level. Unfortunately, disruption of the learning model will not be initiated at the college level. As we discussed in the previous chapter, colleges and universities are being run like corporations. The test 'em, grade 'em, and rank 'em lobby, controlled by politicians and strongly influenced by parents, has a stranglehold on college administrators. College used to serve as the final bridge on the journey from adolescence to young adulthood. Now, colleges have become credentialing services. In a sense, college students are now treated as customers and commodities at the same time.

The "credential" is still important, of course, but it loses its value once you land your first job. As I cited in chapter 4, young people entering the workforce today can expect to have up to thirty jobs over the course of their careers. The superficial nature of the college process, built upon a skill they will never use again—test-taking—

leaves students unprepared for the challenges of a rapidly changing economy where job security is a thing of the past.

It has been alarming to see firsthand how low education leaders have set the bar. Students have been conditioned to pursue goals that are well within their grasp, to earn grades and trophies that become irrelevant after they leave school.

I have been energized and encouraged, however, by my work with students at K–12 schools and colleges across the country. Many of them are tired of being coddled. Quite often, when I challenge young people to reach beyond their grasp by stretching themselves beyond their perceived limitations, their eyes light up. No one has ever challenged them to stretch. It's like, "Wow! Someone actually believes I can do more!" It is a revelation for them.

> *Our education system has not experienced disruption since its inception. A symmetrical learning environment does not prepare young people for an asymmetrical real world.*

In today's economy of rapid change, disruption is the norm. Our education system has not experienced disruption since its inception. A symmetrical learning environment does not prepare young people for an asymmetrical real world. Schools continue to produce Arrivers—young people wired to compare, conform, and settle. Meanwhile, companies are searching for Strivers—people who will adapt, invent, and reinvent their jobs. It is time for education leaders to stand up to the entrenched test 'em, grade 'em, and rank 'em lobby. If they can summon the courage to jettison their antiquated transactional learning model and create an environment that is transformative, our young people will be prepared to strive together in a real world that is perpetually transforming.

CALL TO ACTION

Future generations may look back on this period in our history as the Age of Impression Management. We have become Arriver Nation. Organizations of all types are being built from the outside in. The primary focus of companies, sports organizations, and schools is embellishing and protecting the Brand. We used to brand products like toothpaste. Now we brand people. Remember the old adage, "If you don't stand for something you will fall for anything"? Well, right now, we're falling for a lot. Instead of standing for something, everyone is focused on getting wins, even if they have to lower the bar and redefine winning to do it. Any result will do, whatever it takes to compare favorably with the Competition.

It's time to stop comparing and start competing again. We must rediscover the true meaning of competition, and give it a name that embodies the true essence of what it means to compete: *Strivership*. A spirit of Strivership is built into our nation's DNA. The founding fathers seemed to understand intuitively that an exceptional nation is built not by simply working together, but by striving together. The framers of the Constitution, led by James Madison, embraced an ethos of Stri, rship by establishing a system of checks and balances that essentially created coequal, competing bodies of government.

Our country's first leader, George Washington, embodied a spirit of Striviership. When the Continental Congress wanted someone to lead an army against England—the strongest empire the world had ever known—in the Revolutionary War, Washington didn't blink. When it came time lead a new country mired in uncertainty, Washington was there. And when the framers of the Constitution needed someone to preside over the proceedings to ensure its integrity, he stepped forward.

Fortunately, many of the leaders who followed Washington have sought to emulate his embrace of Striviership, including Abraham Lincoln, who often quoted Washington when confronted with the daunting challenge of leading our country through civil war. These leaders inspired us to stretch beyond what we perceived to be our limitations. JFK challenged us to reach beyond our grasp when he said, "We choose to go to the moon in this decade and do the other things, not because they are easy, but because they are hard."

That challenge was issued more than fifty years ago, when doing things because they were hard was a choice. Product cycles were long and change was incremental. Collaborating, or working together, was enough when efficiency was the key to success. Striving together was the key to staying *ahead of the game*. Now, companies are driven by productivity. Striving together is required to *stay in the game*!

Unlike past generations, we can't afford to wait for the next great leader to arrive on the scene this time. Conventional wisdom holds that you automatically become a leader when you assume a supervisory role with direct reports. But in a world where the only constant is exponential change, the leader-follower paradigm does not work. Now is a time when *everyone* must lead!

Become part of a return to Striver Nation. Seize opportunities to lead by striving together in all of your relationships.

Instead of looking for someone else to inspire you to stretch, look inward and summon the courage to assert a strong sense of self. Move out of your comfort zone to accept the challenge of inventing, adapting, and reinventing your job.

Instead of holding back to protect your brand, actively contribute to your team by standing up for what you believe and by constructively challenging your teammates. If you hold back, you will be robbing your team of learning. Supporting your teammates is crucial, but make earning the respect of your teammates your primary goal. Support offered by simply collaborating to maintain harmonic bliss is superficial. Earn the respect of your teammates by pushing them and by communicating with them directly when an issue arises.

Approach your Relationship to Boss the same way. It's easy to express support, but it only becomes real if you are willing to challenge your boss with new ideas and communicate directly if an issue arises. Without complete transparency, any support you express will be superficial.

If you are in a traditional leadership role, commit to striving together with your direct reports. Leaders *imbue a spirit* by inspiring their direct reports to stretch beyond their perceived limitations. Managers set reachable goals; leaders set goals that challenge their direct reports. Instead of constantly referencing *the goal*, leaders empower their direct reports to focus on the process by cultivating Striver Attributes. Leaders who lead by being led can take a team to unimaginable heights!

Businesses used to be built to last. Now they must be built to invent, adapt, and reinvent. In this disruptive environment, they are in desperate need of Strivers. But the Striver pool is shallow. Our schools, in both athletics and academics, must shed corporatization, get real, and begin to immediately focus on developing Strivers.

People grow when they stretch by putting themselves in situations where they're not sure how things are going to turn out. Take the road less travelled. Build your organization from the inside out. Embrace the tension that comes with a commitment to Strivership. Reach beyond your grasp to achieve beyond expectations! Strive on!